PS

BOOK

by Nick Hobson
Creator of the *Psycards* System

Psycards Illustrations © Maggie Kneen
Psycards © Nick Hobson

PSYCARDS

Published by Psycards Ltd. London
www.psycards.com

In a period of human history when all available energy is spent in the investigation of nature, very little attention is paid to the essence of man, which is his psyche, although many researches are made into its conscious functions. But the really complex and unfamiliar part of the mind, from which symbols are produced is still virtually unexplored. It seems almost incredible that though we receive signals from it every night, deciphering these communications seems too tedious for any but a very few people to be bothered with it. Man's greatest instrument, his psyche, is little thought of, and it is often directly mistrusted and despised. 'It's only psychological' too often means: It is nothing.

Carl Gustav Jung (1875–1961),
Approaching the Unconscious

Things out of perfection sail,
And all their swelling canvas wear,
Nor shall the self-begotten fail
Though fantastic men suppose
Building-yard and stormy shore,
Winding-sheet and swaddling-clothes.

W. B. Yeats (1865–1939)

2012 Edition © Psycards Ltd

The moral right of the author has been asserted. All rights reserved. Without limiting the rights under copyright reserved above, no part of this publication may be reproduced, stored or introduced into a retrieval system, or transmitted, in any form or by any means (electronic, mechanical, photocopying, recording or otherwise), without the prior permission of both the copyright holder and the publisher of this book

Psycards Ltd, 2 Daleham Mews, London, NW3 5DB
www.psycards.com

ISBN 978-0-9532199-0-2

Contents

Introduction

L ike so much it started with a dream. In the early 1980s I was, after a marital quarrel, turned out of the house (probably deservedly). I recall it as a period of pain and turmoil and the collapse of a marriage. I found myself in a friend's spare bedroom tossing and turning on a decidedly sleep-hostile mattress. In my dream I was, as it were, on a high place, looking down on my own life, and could see all the elements that had made me what I was, set out separately: the influences of my family, my background, my education, my friends, my fears, my hopes, my failures, spread out before me like fields in the plain below. My life then was not one undifferentiated blur; it was sharp, with all the component parts separate. The feeling I had was one of peace and control; it was my life, and comprehensible. When I woke, I decided to try to put this personal vision into some form so that others could share it.

Poetry and psychology have always been the things that stirred me from my teens. Jung fascinated me; the poetry of W.B. Yeats, too, had etched itself into my mind. I knew nothing or little about tarot cards. But I sought to work with a system of detachable symbols that could be connected like Lego bricks. So Psycards were born. I strove to create the architecture for simplified blocks of symbols that might reflect the rich complex variety of the psyche and to sketch out the shapes and patterns that would emerge from our unconscious. I was of course lucky (or was it luck?) to find a young illustrator. Her name was Maggie Kneen. She had studied intensively the imagery of Celtic and Anglo-Saxon art. She helped me flesh out in vibrant colours the imagery of the Psycard pack.

Never did I seek to treat Psycards as a commercial cow to be exploited, though it needed to pay its way. Over the last 16 years it has sold steadily. Customers write to say that they bought their pack five years ago and it is looking a bit dog-eared because they have been using it every day. Psycards have a small number of devotees to whom the cards mean a lot. I am happy with that. They are sold in a small way round the world; in the US, Australia and India. One book has been written on Psycards, *The Language of Psycards* by Bernice, which is unfortunately out of print and I offer my respects to it. I believe and hope Psycards are not a fad, but that they will last because they reflect psychic truths.

Telling the Future

Are things pre-destined? Do some people have psychic gifts which enable them to peer into the shape of tomorrow? Which methods work best – astrology, tarot, tea-leaves, crystal balls, even Psycards? These are some of the questions this brief chapter poses.

The idea that the minutiae of our lives, including the breakfast cereal we will be eating, are pre-ordained and written down by God in a huge book, is faintly ridiculous. Many people find comfort in it because, if it is all decided, the agony and the indecision is unnecessary. Calvinists believe (or used to believe) that God destines one soul for salvation and another for damnation and that if you are one of the elect it doesn't matter what you do. Mechanistic psychology, too, says that we all respond to stimuli of pain and pleasure governed by ultimate random chance and that impersonal evolutionary processes make us what we are, and that our DNA will decide when and in which ward of which hospital we will end up.

Kismet, blind chance, our genes, the wheel of fate spinning its roulette ball and dispensing piles of chips of happiness to a lucky few, is not really a world many of us can be happy in. It does not square with what is in our heads. We know we are important. We know we ourselves and others do matter, and that we inhabit a moral universe. The belief that God knows all but that individuals have complete freedom of choice is something theologians and philosophers have struggled to reconcile. Psycards work on the assumption that every individual is precious and has critical choices for good and evil, and happiness and misery, and that it matters to get the choices right.

That does not mean total freedom. We are not like snooker balls on an infinite table that can go anywhere. We are governed by constraints, by our genetic inheritance, maybe our star signs, our family backgrounds, our environment, our historical times and, yes, chance too takes a role. Having said that, each of us starts with a unique individuality that can find its potential or, it may be, not. We are a seed that can find the right soil and grow, or wither. Because we are intelligent we have some influence on how we grow. Psycards' main function is to enhance self-awareness, to make people see what is inside themselves. Only by understanding ourselves can we see and shape our futures.

But a dilemma arises. Because experience tells us

that some people do have uncanny and accurate insight into other people's futures. Psychic gifts are transmitted (it seems to be from mother to daughter) in some families just as clearly as musical talents in others. In the past it was taken for granted that there were things unseen, spirits and powers beyond the grave, and today we grapple with balancing the paranormal with our rational scientific world view. Because we live in a world that is so sceptical of the spiritual world many people suppress their psychic gifts. The psychoanalytic movement of the last hundred years that started with Freud's 'discovery' of the unconscious has given a scientific gloss to the unseen world, which was not regarded as respectable.

Perhaps, then, it is best to think of a broad spectrum of psychic and psychological and psychother-apeutic gifts. At one end there will always be 'seers', with uncanny oracular abilities to see time present and time future intertwined. (Of course there are many others who claim them and some who are fraudulent.) They may use many aids for their gifts: the tarot, crystals, or whatever. At the other end there are dedicated, wise and learned doctors, specialists and teachers who are supported by accepted bodies of knowledge. In the middle there is a large number of people who combine people-skills with intuition. Sensitivity is the defining factor. Common observation tells us that some people have antennae which make them very aware of what is in other people's heads. They can read signals that others miss. They can listen to tones of voice and tiny pulses and set them in a context of experience. They can see inside people and inside themselves. Psycards are for those people who inhabit that broad territory which is bordered on one side by psychic insights and on the other side by psychological understanding.

Psycards and the Tarot

Psycards are seen as a modern, simplified, user-friendly version of the tarot, and many experienced 'readers' find them a useful tool for divination. When asked why, they reply that the cards offer clear channels for psychic energy and are powerful transmitters. They enable their clients to react quickly. But Psycards do not seek to be a 'me-too' tarot pack – although they share four of the tarot major Arcana Cards.

The tarot is mysterious. It is meant to be. It is ancient. Nobody really knows how it started and when. It surfaced some five hundred years ago with the origin of printing. With the twenty-two major Arcana Cards and the fifty-six minor Arcana that started the suits of today's playing cards, it may have originated as a game. It caught on in the late eighteenth century at a time when the mysteries of the East, and Egypt in particular, were attracting intellectuals who had supped too long on an Enlightenment diet. Tarot has roots that have been entwined with the Kabbala, with the Sufis perhaps, and the whole European mystical tradition. The names of the cards – the Priestess, the Chariot, the Emperor – tell us of a fifteenth-century Catholic Europe that was bubbling with new forces. Maybe the tarot was cocking a snook at the priests. Maybe it was sneaking in some of the heretical Eastern themes that the Church had suppressed in the Albigensian Crusade. Maybe it was a mnemonic or memory system to remind devotees of inner paths and disciplines. Maybe it tapped even older roots. It's the maybes that make the tarot so fascinating. It is esoteric and it usually needs to be interpreted by a 'reader' or demands a steep learning curve.

Psycards aims to be direct and accessible. It draws on elements of the psychoanalytic movement, the poets of the twentieth century, fairy stories and myths that are threaded through our culture. Psycards hopes to speak to people without the mediation of the interpreter. Tarot, as it were, needs a priestly interpreter, whereas Psycards puts in vernacular language the mysteries of the heart.

The Power of Symbols

Psycards work through the power of symbols. A symbol is something that stands for something else. It's a signpost as it were. The plus sign (+) is an example, indeed the word 'table' represents the whole object. Humans work all the time with symbols and that is one of the ways we're different from animals. Some symbols are arbitrary; but others are purely personal (e.g. the tie she gave me) but others have a power and meaning for the generality of men and women. Symbols are the stuff of dream, religion, poetry, drama and art, and finds themselves into every branch of human affairs.

How do they work? Let's take an example. A lighted candle. From our birthday parties to romantic dinners, from Christmas trees to altars and ceremonies we all have reactions to a candle. We can see the fat bud of light, and feel the dripping wax, and the perilous way it sways in a puff of wind. It evokes personal memories from each of us. We can all think of phrases and pictures with candles in. We think of times when the electricity fails. A candle then can and does say lots of things to us: hope, the frailty and preciousness of human life, the divine spark, romance, Christmas, togetherness, loneliness, the male organ. You don't need to spell out all the complex associations. A candle like any other powerful symbol acts like a magnet which attracts to us feelings and memories and connections.

A symbol like this works on different levels: intellectual and emotional. Over the years, maybe for hundreds and thousands of years, individual powerful symbols have worked themselves into the wiring of our brains.

A symbol is a bridge (yes, a bridge is another symbol) that links two different areas of human experience. The candle can be a link between the sexy dinner date and a church ceremony. It can connect the everyday with the spiritual level and the conscious with the unconscious. It has a passport to travel anywhere, in dreams, in poems, in advertisements, in Old Masters, comics, TV Soaps, the High Altar and witches' covens.

Symbols too are pictures or images that a child can draw with a crayon. They are concrete not abstract, and because they are more than words you cannot disapprove of them or argue with them. So they can exert a pull on the whole person rather than just the head, They are attractive; your eyes are drawn to them.

Symbols work fast just because they are words and pictures combined. An idea in words takes time to ingest and your critical faculties have time to come into action, whereas a symbol can be swallowed without chewing like a sugar-coated pill.

Symbols cannot be owned. The Nazis might have appropriated the swastika which is not a true symbol, but symbols are ambivalent. They mean a lot to people, but they have different meanings for different people, They are like fish who dart away in the unconscious ocean, or diamonds that flash from different aspects. You cannot quite nail them down.

Symbols point upwards. One of the key beliefs of symbolism is 'as above so below'. This says that the earth is mirrored -if darkly – with heaven. Symbolism draws on Neo-Platonist philosophy which teaches of an ideal world which we can aspire to. Symbols are ladders that can move from one to another.

Bridges... passports... sugar-coated pills... fishes... diamonds... ladders. Maybe we should not apologise for the abundance of metaphors. That is the way symbols work. Psycards seek to present and structure many of the powerful symbols that are threaded through our culture.

Approaching the cards

This is an overview of the 40 cards in the Psycard pack with some basic pointers on how to work with them. Towards the end of the book you will find an extended chapter entitled 'Using the Psycards'

Why 40 Cards?

How can one compress the rich complexity of psychological, emotional, philosophical. personal and practical insights – the Wisdom of the Ages – into 40 separate bits of cardboard with pictures on?

Well, of course, one can't. Psycards seek to pick elements of myth, religion, folk wisdom and psychoanalytic theory into a comprehensible and accessible system. One reason it ends with up with 40 cards is manage-ability. If you are lost and looking for a direction you want a street map rather than carry around twenty volumes of *Encyclopaedia Britannica*. An over-weighty cargo can swamp the frail boat of the psyche. (Not to mention the dimensions of the table you need to spread double the number of cards!) Each card is a signpost to vast tracts on inner territory. Many have multiple layers of meaning. Many are pegs for you to hang your own associations on. The 40 Cards need to reflect what is in you and the system stands or falls on how meaningful they are to you.

The Groupings of the Cards

The cards are grouped into five main categories: Direction Cards, Fundamentals, Symbols, Archetypes, Characters and Happenings.

The Inquirer

The Inquirer stands for you if you are consulting the cards for yourself or the person whom you are counselling or for whom you are doing a reading. When you shuffle the cards you will watch the ones nearest to the Inquirer because they show the strongest influence.

The Direction Cards

These cards point directly to action and can give you straightforward answers to questions you ask. They also act as a sort of punctuation. Two or three cards leading up to a direction show a sequence of thought that culminates in a course for action. They can also reinforce and echo your inner intentions. But note they can act as a mocking voice or sometimes an alternative whisper and you need to be alert to the tone of voice of the card.

The Fundamentals

These seven cards relate to those elements of our lives that are common to each of us and nearest to our daily existence. They are the foundation of our well being and reflect background and environmental influences.

The Archetypes

These seven cards depict underlying forces which go to shape our make-up. Common to us all, they reflect landmarks of the individual's life span. Ingrained within our psyches they are archetypal – part of our psychological wiring.

The Symbols

These cards portray seven powerful symbols that have governed hearts and minds for thousands of years. They are universal and occur in myth and legend and are encrusted with rich associations, and have a relevance to personality types and psychological moods.

The Characters

If our life is a play here are some of the characters who walk across the stage. They reflect different aspects of others and ourselves. You need to relate them to real people including yourself, bearing that we play different parts in our lives and we have multiple elements in our personalities.

The Happenings

Things happen in our lives. They may be bubbling up from inside us; they may be the results of random forces from outside; they may be caused by the intervention of others. These cards seek to alert us to those events we are pre-disposed to receive, or are latent within us or our environment. They are happenings that can transform our lives and our psychology.

Upside Downside

Psycards are designed to be read with the image upright. In Tarot some people assign an opposite meaning for an upside down card. With Psycards its is suggested when you turn over the cards that you turn them to an upright position.

Reading the Cards

The basic rule of Psycards is that, while each card has a power and influence in its own right, its influence is modified by those cards near it. Think of it in different ways: like each card having an aura that radiates to nearby cards; or a radio transmitter with a sound footprint; or with a strong colour that blends with one next to it to create a new colour; or a flavour that transforms a dish. It is up to you, the reader, to pick up the signals by making connections in your mind to create a meaning and a pattern. As well as emitting energy the card is receiving it. It is pulsing like a heart in a rhythm of systole and diastole.

Usually the cards are spread and read in linear patterns which define certain directions for meaning to travel:

Reading from left to right denotes development from past through present to future. From below to above denotes movement up from the unconscious, the hidden, the dark, the underlying towards the conscious, up to fulfilment, goals, and aspirations and perhaps to spiritual perfection. (Like a plant growing from its roots in the soil up to its flower and its fruit.)

You can also look for circular energy flows and meaning and here the flow goes anti-clockwise. In the final chapter there are a number of defined spreads, and you, of course, can create your own.

Your 'Night Sky' Reading

Psycards asks you to make meaningful connections between cards and here is a suggestion for one way to approach the cards for the first time. (There is an alternative way in the last chapter.)

Shuffle the pack and deal the cards in eight rows of five, face upwards.

Imagine you were looking at the sky on a clear

night with a myriad of stars, some in clusters, some in straight lines, some throbbing. In the same way let your eyes make some shapes with the cards. Look for the Inquirer. Note what is above and below, and left and right of it. Ask what signals it could mean for you. Look then for any combination of two or three cards adjoining that are of any significance to you. Relax. Let your imagination play. Don't expect the voice of destiny, but listen for a few quiet inner whispers....

1

THE INQUIRER

Know yourself the sages say
Out of the maze you'll find your way

ThisisthestartofthePsycardpack.Itis essentially about you, the person asking the questions. (Or the person on behalf of whom you are giving a reading.) It is the I, 'I'nquiring. It indicates that you are asking for guidance and clarification.

This is one of the few cards that does not have an easily identifiable pictorial symbol. The formal intricate pattern is perhaps a maze – like the one at Hampton Court. At the heart of it is an Elizabethan knot. Knots and mazes … it tells us we must find a way out of the complex labyrinth that is our own inner life and untie some of the mysteries within ourselves. The picture reflects the two sides of darkness and light, because life is always opposites; a dialectic, an argument between day and night, yin and yang, good and evil. The colours, predominantly green, ask for control and contemplation. The formal design is deliberate.

The Inquirer Card tells us that we are embarking on a journey of inner knowledge. At the Oracle at Delphi in Ancient Greece the words 'Know Yourself' were inscribed because any understanding of our hopes and futures and the healing of ourselves has to come from self-awareness. When the card occurs it reminds us that we are seekers of truth, explorers of our own inner psychic landscape. It demands honesty and humility. It tells us to be open to new ideas. Another way of looking at the Inquirer card is to think of your own life, or that of the person on whose behalf you are reading, as a fairy story. The card says 'Once Upon a Time'. You are the hero or the heroine, and wonderful adventures and mysterious characters will meet you on the road.

The concept of the inquirer goes through poetry and our culture. When Dante made his journey into the infernal regions he was such an inquirer. The mediaeval alchemists saw their search for turning metal into gold as a spiritual quest demanding, above all, humility.

Psychoanalysts from Freud onwards have submitted themselves to analysis on their own psychic makeup. Mozart's opera *The Magic Flute* contains the same message; find yourself and transform yourself.

This, of course, means transcending the ego. The Ego is bossy. In many cases it seeks to edge out the other parts of your nature. The wise seeker will not just let the Ego dominate.

Look again at the card. Does not the central knot remind you of the eye, the dispassionate eye? Or is it like a peephole through a door through which you can see into a beautiful garden?

Mix the cards. Watch carefully the cards that fall on either side, above or below the Inquirer Card. They can alert you to the forces that are affecting the Inquirer's life. Wherever it occurs, let it remind you too of the seriousness of your psychic quest.

ASSOCIATIONS AND OPPOSITES

The Searcher	The quest
The 'I' and 'You'	'We' and 'They'
The psychic maze	
Looking inside yourself	The Material World
Introversion	Extroversion
Exploring	Knowing all the answers
Self awareness	The Bossy Ego
Once Upon a Time...	Humility
Listening	Talking

THOUGHT PROMPTS

❖ Do you think you can understand other people without understanding yourself?

❖ How would you tell your own life story as if it were a fairy story?

❖ Do you think it is better to undertake a journey of inner understanding alone or with a companion or guide?

❖ How can the Inquirer best prepare him or herself before embarking on an inner journey?

2

YES

Don't shilly shally. With full speed
This card commands you to proceed

You are driving up to a busy road junction in a fast line of cars. To avoid collisions your eyes are fixed on the traffic lights. The Yes Card is your green light. Life is about making choices. You cannot dilly dally on some occasions. This card is one of the Indicator Cards that seek to help you make decisions. They work in conjunction with cards and sequences, and come into play when you want to ask specific questions that can be answered by a yes and a no.

This, like the Inquirer Card, is a non-symbolic card. Strong shades of blue with a splash of flowers and lattice work. The reds and cobalt blues convey vitality and purpose, pointing the reader to action.

The reason that the Yes Card is in the Psycard pack reflects a basic truth about life and how we operate. Whether at an everyday level, or at critical times we all have to make choices and decisions. We may have imperfect information at our disposal; we may feel there is an equal balance of pro's and con's. But there is no evasion possible of our necessity to jump one way or the other.

In this situation there is no substitute for 'Will' – your courage to make a choice. Shall I marry that person? Shall I take that job? Shall I buy that house? You make your life and your destiny is made up with the choices you have made, just as your body is made up of the food you eat. The Yes Card helps you take that plunge.

'There is a tide in the affairs of men, when taken at the flood leads on to fortune. Omitted, all the voyage of their life is bound in shallows and in miseries.' What Shakespeare says is echoed by the existentialists who see each individual finding their freedom by making choices – often blind choices.

The Yes Card is also about taking a positive attitude to life. It is better to open doors to new experiences and new people than to shut them. Growth depends upon, taking risks, whereas caution means you incur the danger of wilting and being left on the sidelines. The power of positive thinking is more than a catchphrase. It is a mental attitude that can be learned and can change yourself and how people react to you. Optimism is a much more successful strategy than pessimism. If you expect good things happen your attitude makes those good things actually to happen. Luck comes to people who smile. Confidence generates confidence. The Yes Card is telling you that you can oil the wheels of all the beneficial cycles in your favour.

The Yes Card sends its message to you either by itself or in conjunction with other cards. You can use it as a day to day guide. Shall I phone John? Shall I go to that party? Shall I speak to the boss? You can turn up the Psycards one by one and if the Yes Card appears before the No card your decision is made. But that is perhaps to treat it as too superficial. In conjunction with other cards it helps transmit energy flows from one, to another, leading you on to new paths. After the Message Card you see the Yes Card and after that the Beauty Card. Yes, it says phone her up. That sort of sequence leads you on to explore the next cards.

You can think of the Yes Card as an outside voice telling you to 'do this', 'do that'. But think of it also as an inner voice, pleading like a neglected child, pointing to the card next door to it, saying 'Yes, let's do that instead.'

The Yes Card is good news. It is affirmation and confidence. It should reinforce the psychological bias you have to any specific course of action.

ASSOCIATIONS AND OPPOSITES

Positive Attitudes	Negativity
Green lights	Red lights
Full speed ahead	Being stuck in a lay-by
The courage to make choices	
Smiling at life	Scowling at life
Your will power	
Acceptance of life	
Alertness to symbols	Dilly dallying
Optimism	Pessimism
Accepting the universe	
Daring to act	Moaning

THOUGHT PROMPTS

❖ Can you think back to how you made a key decision at one stage of your life?
❖ Can you think of somebody you know who has the power to make fast decisions?
❖ Can you think of somebody whose life is open and affirmative and whose attitude brings about results?
❖ Can you think of somebody in a story who dared to say 'yes' to a great opportunity?

3

NO

If you're in doubt about the track
This card commands you to go back

The No Card is the mirror card of the Yes Card and much of the same applies. It is there to help you make decisions in specific situations, and in conjunction with other cards gives you messages about proceeding along certain lines of thinking.

It is an abstract card. Here the reds and blues are used to give negative overtones.

'No' is of course one of the most painful words in the language. Can I stay up tonight? Will you lend me £10? Can I join your group? 'No' is all too often a slap in the face. But it is also necessary. No, you cannot play with electric wires. No, that colour doesn't suit you. No, we wouldn't be happy together.

So the No Card is very often a strong card and must be heeded. If you go careering through red lights you'll have a crash. If your energies are being diverted into sterile courses it's necessary to have the road blocked. Remember too that timing is all. Traffic lights that are red will turn to green. And don't forget that the No Card is not 'Destiny Calling', or a flaming sword keeping you out of paradise. It is often a quiet inner whisper of negativity – of your self backing away from a course of action.

Growth in your inner life, just like elsewhere, depends on energy flows. If one avenue is closed another opens. A gardener pruning a rose bush has to say no to many stems in order to achieve abundant foliage. Sometime a stream has to be dammed if it is to turn the generators of the power plant. So it takes courage and decisiveness to say no in many situations.

So as in the Yes Card there are two ways to look at the No Card. You can use it in those situations where a decision simply has to be made and you cannot sit on the fence.

There are certain techniques and stages for saying no. You can note your gut reaction – which may reflect your inner feelings. You should double check that emotionally as well as rationally you really do want to say no. And once you've thought about it you should be firm. Say no loud and clear. Let your body language back it up. Don't back down in the face of inevitable complaints.

There is another way of looking at the card. It can on occasions denote that negativity that rejects life.

When the No Card occurs in sequences, take note of the flow of the cards in front of it. The Body Card followed by the Voyage Card followed by the No Card might be asking you to think twice about your health on holiday. The Money Card next to the Home Card next to No could make you think twice about increasing your mortgage.

So don't think the No Card is always bad news. It tells you to change course. It warns you against negative thinking that saps your precious energies. It strengthens your will and reinforces it when you have already a psychological bias against any specific course of action.

ASSOCIATIONS AND OPPOSITES

A red flashing warning	Ploughing on to disaster
Rejecting temptation	Going downhill
Negative Attitudes to life	Positive thinking
Rejecting	Being rejected
A sharp break	A chance for new growth
Making painful decisions	Letting things slide
Saying 'no' in words but not in body language	Confusing signals

THOUGHT PROMPTS

- ❖ When did you last have the courage to say 'no' to somebody?
- ❖ When did someone last say 'no' to you?
- ❖ Can you think of figures in politics or history or in your own experience who said 'no' — and with what consequences?
- ❖ Do you know someone whose life has been blighted by negative attitudes and who radiates negative energies?

4

NOW

The hour is ripe. Now is your hour
Go to fulfil your heart's desire

This is still one of the four Direction Cards that provide help to interpret the meaning of other cards, and that act as punctuation to a sequence of cards. The Now Card tells you of ripeness and immediacy and it is strong, direct and positive.

The picture is, as it were, of a stained glass window with ornamental blue and orange panels. In the top right hand corner the sun is shining upon a farmer who is cutting the corn with a scythe and binding it in sheaves – as farmers did in the time-old ways before agricultural revolutions. The corn is the bread of life that he has sowed. Now in the summer the harvest can be stored.

The message for the reader is that the time is ripe for you in aspects of either your inner or your outer life, and the climate is right to act.

Important energies never go in straight lines. They work in cyclical rhythms that mirror the seasons of the year. There is a time in our lives for sowing seeds and a time to harvest them. In other words we have always psychological 'windows' we need to exploit. If we fail to cut the corn in our field, it will rot and we will starve. So the implication is not that we've won the jackpot. It is instead we have received our just desserts.

'Now' is the moment for action and to stop dreaming. The reality is today. The psychological forces that have been germinating within you are ripe and you must bring them to fruition. Make hay while the sun shines.

There is too a message of gratitude in the Now

Card. The harvest is always the time to be thankful for gifts that we have been given, for the prosperity we may be enjoying. We need to say thank you (just as children) in order to receive good things in the future.

Both the Now Card and the Yes Card are of course favourable and positive signals, but it is worth looking at the ways in which they are different. The Yes Card is about making choices – sometimes on imperfect evidence. You need the will to act in certain situations. The Now Card is gentler. Your instincts tell you there are inherent rhythms that are impelling you to act.

It may be helpful is to think of this card as maturity. There is a natural time for children to leave home. Children turn into teenagers. A long relationship matures into marriage and there is a critical point when it is ready for it. There is a right time to change careers or move jobs or start a new venture, because your whole experience is building up for that to happen. Be prepared too for what may seem fortuitous coincidences. Within our lives two or three separate lines can converge and offer us exciting opportunities.

'Ripeness is all' as Shakespeare says. The 'Now' Card alerts us that the time has come in our life.

ASSOCIATIONS AND OPPOSITES

Immediacy	Delaying
Ripeness	Underdeveloped – or over ripe
Coming to fruition	Stalling
Opportunity knocks	Putting things on the back burner
Natural development	Forcing things too early
The key point in a relationship	Miss it – and it dies on you
The moment of truth	Missing the boat
Gratitude to life	Not saying thank you
Heaven sent chances	Being blind to your good fortune
The rhythms of life	Mechanistic approach to decisions
Now	Never

THOUGHT PROMPTS

❖ Recall some of the occasions when things were ripe in your life.

❖ Do you know people who missed opportunities that never recurred?

❖ Do you know any characters in TV, books or films who exemplify the quality of ripeness?

5

NEVER

*Never delude yourself. This must
Bring a treasured dream to dust*

This is the last of the Direction Cards and is the opposite in many senses of the Now Card. Its message is cold and bleak. It tells you a door has been shut.

In the picture a raven is set in the wintry snow. The raven is black, almost funereal. Nature's ravens do not qualify for lovability. 'Ghastly, grim and ancient raven wandering from the Nightly shore,' said Edgar Allen Poe, Take thy beak, and take thy form from off my door!

Quote the Raven 'Nevermore'.

That is why this card is so illustrated. On the No Card we said the word 'no' can come like a slap in the face. It can close a road to encourage you to divert to another. The Never Card seeks to rid you of illusions. It tells us it is psychologically damaging to cling to a dead dream. There are habits and relationships in our lives which are destitute and we need to break away and this is alerting us to this. It says reality can be cruel, but in order to grow we have to accept finality. We all come across barriers on occasions. An example of this might be of the card warning to us to break finally from an addiction (Some people can be as bad for us as some drugs!)

Breaking away from illusions brings depression and a feeling of failure. The card can sometimes be warning you not to destroy other people's illusions. There is always a fine line between giving honest advice to people and stripping them of the necessary element of illusion and beliefs that support their hopes. Not only may you be wrong (which is always possible for us all) but you may be destroying a human being. It is the story of Ibsen's play *The Wild Duck*.

The Never Card can stand (like the Cave Card) for those periods of depression that will alternate in many of us who have a temperament that oscillates from happiness to gloom.

As the poet Yeats says,

There through the broken branches go
The ravens of unresting thought
Flying crying to and fro.

So the card can stand for 'Black Dog' as Winston Churchill called his moods of depression. It can alert us to a feeling of negativity that is blighting everything we do.

The Raven is a scavenger. It is looking for any emotional carcasses in your life and maybe in other people's lives. Maybe we can think of it as an undertaker disposing of some of the dead parts that need purging.

The Never Card is one where it makes particular sense to look at the adjoining cards to find its relevance. Look for the Peace Card. Is it nearby? It tells us that spiritual tranquillity is at hand. The Serenity prayer which says 'God grant me serenity to accept the things I cannot change, the courage to change things I can and the wisdom to know the difference.' Again, as with the Yes and No Card, the Never Card is also about taking responsibility for our lives, creating what we want but also accepting the inevitable.

ASSOCIATIONS AND OPPOSITES

Finality	Acceptance of reality
Lack of fulfilment	Destroying illusions
The end of a bad relationship	The chance to give new growth
Breaking habits and daring to stop …	
Having the courage to change life-style	
Scavenging on other people	
Enjoying other people's weakness	Depression
Moods changes	Funerals
The hope for a new life	
The Dark Night of the Soul	Dawn
Restless unhappy thoughts	Tranquillity

THOUGHT PROMPTS

❖ Do you know anyone who changed a habit or a lifestyle? What caused that?

❖ Do you know people who need illusions in order to continue their lives? Is it in those cases right to puncture these illusions?

❖ Do people say 'Nevermore' to a person or habit of their own accord or do outside events force them to do it?

❖ Can you think of a situation in the life of a celebrity or character in a 'soap' where the Never Card would be appropriate?

6

THE BODY

*Blood and bone and living cell
Builds this holy temple well*

You are inside the marvel of the Universe. The organs, functions and control systems of this factory are designed to make one priceless and unique product: you. The Body Card is the first card in the Psycard pack of the 'Fundamentals'. They are central to the make-up of each one of us as individuals. They focus on one of the central components of our lives. This card is about our physicality and our health and it has symbolic meanings beyond that.

We see a figure, arms and legs outstretched with the muscles and the veins showing through the skin. The basic colour is the radiant blue of healing and the red of the vital forces. It depicts the medians and energy flows on which Chinese medicine is based. The image reflects the Michelangelo drawing of the proportions of Man. Yet it is essentially a-sexual.

Perhaps the first message of the card is to remind us we are body-bound and to be thankful for it. We are fuelled by pleasure and the functions of breathing, sucking, eating, ingesting, secreting and excreting are the background music against which our lives are lived. Our bodies are to be stroked, hugged and loved. They are for warmth and generosity. So the Body Card tells us that there are times that touching can solve human problems that words cannot.

The messages this card sends to us are many-sided. Primarily it must be about health. Mind, body and spirit are interconnected. The body gives us information about our overall health, which can be interpreted as balance and wholeness. (Health and Wholeness have the same word origin.). Body cannot be divorced from mind or spirit. So the Body Card is telling you that you should seek an equipoise in your life.

Health too is linked to diet. Can it point us to a regimen in our lifestyle? Psycards can tell us some blazingly obvious things, and if the Body Card was sitting next to the Scales Card, who would not wonder if they should be dieting. Physical exercise is necessary for our health. Is the card telling us to introduce more balance between work and play? Bodies have needs and urges for love and sex and closeness. We should ask what relevance it has for us.

Our bodies are about physicality and flesh abhors abstractions. Imposing idealised shapes on male and female bodies are always a distortion of nature. The Body Card asks us to be tolerant for the bulges and blemishes of others and ourselves. An over-obsession with the body is an imbalance. Hypochondria is not healthy. Someone who pumps iron or spends a long time with the manicurist could be justifiably criticised for allowing the body to overshadow the important sides of their psyche, just as a couch-potato is imbalanced.

Linked to the body is the concept of rhythm which points to dance and music, and this card should remind us of the role they need to play in our lives. We need to listen to the inner music of our bodies: its biorhythms, its menstrual cycles, the circulation of the blood, the moods that are triggered by the seasons, and the birth and death of our cells.

Our bodies talk to those around us. Body language manifests itself in our posture, our gestures, our stance. Your own body speaks. Stop now and for thirty seconds listen to your own body. Can you hear it has its own message for you?

ASSOCIATIONS AND OPPOSITES

Health	Sickness
Diet	
Wholeness	
An interconnected system	
Pleasure and sensations	Pain
Closeness and touch	
Warm and hugging	Coldness
Body language	
Physicality	Abstraction
Function	Malfunction

THOUGHT PROMPTS

❖ Are women more concerned with their bodies than men? If so why?
❖ Why are some people 'physical' and other not ?
❖ Why is it that some people touch others naturally and easily ? Do some people resent being touched?
❖ Do you like your own body?
❖ How much does the shape of someone's body tell you about their personality and their soul?

7

HOME

As every sparrow seeks its nest
Fly to yours to seek your rest

'The foxes have holes and the birds in the air have nests…' And what about you? This card tells you of your need for security and stability. The second of the Fundamentals is the Home Card. Where we live – fundamental to our own make-up or that of anyone we seek to understand.

The picture tells us of warmth and comfort, it is a dream of childhood perhaps. Maybe it reminds us of coming in for tea after school, where there is a welcoming fire, a cat on the mat, two mugs (because there has to be someone to listen to us) on the table. Of course it is old fashioned. Home is. We can all smell the mysterious and beautiful smells of home … polish, cooking fresh bread, laundry, warmth.

The card is reminding us of our origins. It is ambivalent. Were we happy? Do we seek to re-create it? Were we always trying to escape from its suffocating constraints of families and siblings?

So this card is allowing us to go back to our roots. We all have feelings of home whether happy or unhappy. One's memory goes back to our first teddy bear, the wallpaper in the bedroom and with it memories we seek to forget. And for some people who have moved up in life the Home Card may bring them back with a jolt to their origins. They were not born star children spangled with success: like the rest of us they were nurtured in nappies. For them the message is to bring a degree of humility.

Some of us idealise our childhood. Our homes were broken or may have been riven by unhappy parents or poverty or abuse of one sort or another, and we have managed to put a gloss on it. The Home Card tells us to re-live it again in order to maybe grow out of it.

Our homes are safety and security, and the card is asking us whether we are using the home as a bolt hole or fortress to protect ourselves against a hostile outside world. At some times in our lives, when we are in a 'nesting' phase, we are home-conscious. When we are trying to fly the coop or ejecting fledglings the warmth and attraction of home fades. The Home Card asks us which cycle of our lives we are in.

'Home is where the heart is' goes the saying. We are being reminded to think of what really matters to us all. Everybody has a homing instinct that leads them to head in one direction when there is trouble. For some men maybe it is the pub. For others it is the village where they were born. Others nurse their wounds in their job. The Home Card is asking us where we are 'earthed'.

Psycards also reminds us of the direct and immediate things in our lives. So the Home Card can point us to the physical place where we live now. Few of us live in cardboard boxes or monasteries. We instead live within bricks and mortar with roofs that leak, with a mortgage debt that never seems to decrease. Home-work cannot be ignored. Home-makers (some decades ago there were people called housewives) have a necessary role, and maybe the card is alerting us to its importance.

So the Home Card is asking us to focus on the

importance we place on where we live now, and the cards lying in proximity to it alert us to various possibilities. Sometimes the Work Card may show there is conflict between them. Maybe the Skills Card and the Work Card may suggest the idea of starting a business at home.

Some of us are 'homey' people – pastoralists who are happier tilling our own fields; others are wanderers…nomads. These latter may have a spiritual home, and they may have roots deep inside themselves.

ASSOCIATIONS AND OPPOSITES

Our origins and background	
Our childhood	
Bricks and mortar	
Domesticity	
	A nomad or gypsy life
Homey-ness	
	Voyaging
Safety, security, stability	Danger
Nostalgia	
Being earthed and anchored	Being lost
Being house-proud	Sluttish-ness
Nesting instincts	

THOUGHT PROMPTS
❖ Can you remember in details the kitchen of the home where you were brought up?
❖ Does being a home-oriented person mean you are less interested in the outside world?
❖ Are men in your experience less interested in houses than women?
❖ Do you have more home-making skills than your parents? Are they instinctual or taught?

8

WORK

*Fortunate you in life to find
True reward in daily grind*

Is there something you ought to do? This rather serious card asks you what your duties and responsibilities are. Another of the Fundamentals Card is Work. From childhood till we die we have things to do and these tasks are central to our happiness. This card helps us to evaluate this in our personal mix.

The picture shows cogs and wheels and pulleys in a piece of complex machinery; maybe it is like the inside of a grandfather clock, maybe some antiquated factory. The card asks a question. Is your work a grind?

Adam was cast out of the Garden of Eden and had to earn his bread by the sweat of his brow. The world has changed. Children are not sent down mines. The working week is around 40 hours. Those of us who are in jobs consider ourselves lucky. We still have to work in order to live and prosper. Work can mean a back-breaking day on a construction site or a centrally-heated office. It can be a lonely musician working on a new score, or a mother with a young baby, or a child doing homework. The words 'job', 'function', 'task', 'role' and 'employment' all have different connotations. Being unemployed is destructive to our happiness and confidence. Yet leisure and freedom to do what we want is so often our goal.

So the Work Card asks each of us to put a psychic value on the role of work in our lives, to ask is it truly rewarding in satisfaction terms or just as a pay packet to let us do other things.

The work we do is our identity. We need to ask people what they do to understand them. The Work

Card asks us in relation to ourselves and other people how much work really matters to us. Maybe doing the garden for two hours is more meaningful to us than doing forty hours in a soulless office, and, if so, it is suggested that we change our job. It alerts us all the time to find ways to make work positive for us and not negative. It tells us to question our routines and work patterns.

It can also point us to our place of work and the people within it. Many people marry colleagues at work and their social lives centre round the office or focus on the after-work drink at the pub. The card can remind us of this. Conflict with bosses and people at work are a cause of stress and we need to be psychologically aware of how best to handle these situations. Are you being prompted to consider working in a different way with your colleagues?

Maybe the Work Card is telling you that you are turning into a 'work-aholic' and that other aspects of your life are being neglected. That is perhaps a bit different from being governed by a 'work-ethic'. Some people have a strong conscientious attitude that puts a high moral value on work. The 'work-ethic' seems to produce success, but being a 'work-aholic' seems to tend more to ulcers.

If you look closely at the card there is a cog in the top left which is detached. Maybe you identify with it. Like you, maybe it is self-employed or self sufficient? The trend to advanced technology encourages the growth of working at home and starting small businesses. This sometimes means the loss of the workplace and the support of the colleagues. If so, you may need a compensating social side and in these cases the adjacent cards can remind you of this.

The Work Card asks us not to be trapped as a cog in the machine. It encourages us to shape work to our own goals.

ASSOCIATIONS AND OPPOSITES

The daily grind	Unemployment
Your job	Duty and responsibility
The tasks you have	Routine
Having no function	Career changes
Dead ends	
Creating something	Feeling alienated
Putting your back into something	Slacking
The people at work	
Friendly work	Lonely work
The economy	
Work when you are in control	Work when you are a cog

THOUGHT PROMPTS

❖ How many different sorts of work do you personally do, including the responsibilities you have to people and families, as well as job-related work?

❖ Do you know people who choose to lead their lives dominated by work so as to avoid to be fully human?

❖ What part does work play in your own social life?

❖ Do you ever see characters on TV in real-life work situations, and without seeing them at work can you really understand them?

9

THE SKILLS

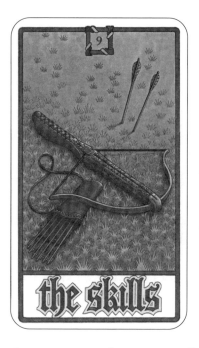

The arrows in the quiver tell
Go use your precious talents well

You are equipped with a bundle of special skills. You need to assess them, sharpen them – and use them to the full. The Skills Card tells you that you have it in you to achieve your targets.

The picture shows a crossbow lying on the ground with a quiver of arrows. The colours are those of vitality and alertness. The archer is practising, and it tells us that we need to use our skills and talents and keep them sharp for those times we need them.

Everyone is gifted in some way. Our genetic endowment as human beings and the specific genes we have inherited puts at our disposal a wealth of skills and talents. Some very young children have a musical gift . Mozart was acclaimed as a genius at the age of five! Physical strength and health are given to some of us. Psychic gifts are transmitted from mother or daughter across the generations. The talents we were born with need to be developed and other skills need to be acquired through our lives. This is what the Skills Card is telling us . At the current state of our lives we need to practise and develop latent skills and learn new ones.

The card is highlighting our own schooling and education and that of others. Were we under-educated or over-educated? Did we use the time properly? Were we properly taught? Are we encouraging those around us to make the most of their schooling ?

Throughout our lives we are on an adventure to overcome obstacles and achieve our goals. We therefore need a range of skills, or arrows in our quiver, or tools in our toolbag. Some we are given. Others we need to acquire on the journey, and all the time we need continually to sharpen up the one we have. So the Skills Card is asking us which are the specific skills we need to handle immediate problems. The proximity of other cards may help us. Maybe the Union Card nearby tells us to use our diplomatic skills to reconcile when there is a conflict looming. Maybe the Message Card nearby tells us we need to apply communication skills.

Education does not stop at eighteen. Today we need to learn new skills all through our lives and past into retirement. Should we take an Adult Education programme to sharpen up some of the neglected arrows in our quiver? Should one buy a book on dog-training? The message is to extend ourselves and sharpen ourselves. The card stands for Self Development and the long journey of personal growth.

Our identity is governed by the skills we possess. Among the Greek gods Apollo was known as a musician and a healer, Vulcan as a smith, Mercury as a messenger. Maybe it makes sense to ask which skill you would be identified with. As a teacher…a chef…an entertainer …a peacemaker?

Another way of looking at the Skills Card is techniques: there are problems in life that can only be overcome by certain techniques. Sexual technique is different from love but it is a skill that can be learnt. There are techniques for handling difficult people, there are techniques for finding inner peace: they can be learnt by meditation. There are arts for growing old and even for dying.

The anthropologists define us as 'homo habilis': clever creatures who learn and transmit techniques to shape axes and build power stations. The Skills Card reminds you that you are clever enough to solve your problems.

ASSOCIATIONS AND OPPOSITES

Skills	Knowing it all
Techniques	
Education	
Closing doors to personal development	
Learning Curves	
Tools and Equipment	
Inherent talent	Wasting talent
Acquired skills	
Schools and Teachers	
Problem Solving	
New hobbies	Vegetating

THOUGHT PROMPTS

❖ Which skills have you acquired since you were at school?
❖ Is it best to learn things out of necessity or is it better to acquire them through an interest?
❖ Can you think of any individual (aside from your family) who taught you a specific skill?
❖ Do you think that emotional and human problems can be solved by techniques?

10

MONEY

Gold from the earth gold from the sky
Gold comes unexpectedly

Sorry, this card does not promise you will win the lottery or inherit a fortune. Psycards tells you about things inside your head and the Money Card seeks to identify your hopes and fears about money.

The picture shows a ploughman earning his crust. In the field where he will soon plough there is – half exposed in the soil – a glint of gold suggesting that a treasure hoard is to be found. The heavy earth...the bare trees of winter ... the grey sky ... the mood of the card is heavy with expectancy. It poses questions. Will the poor ploughman see it? Will he become equally prosperous if he does not find the treasure and continues as a farmer? Is money good for us if it is not earned?

One of the messages that the Money Card is telling us is to plough our own furrow straight and deep, and that the good earth will turn up for us our rewards – perhaps in terms of grain, perhaps in terms of gold.

Often money and wealth will come as a by-product of some other goal that we seek. If you set money as a target you may well not get it. Mammon does not reward all his devotees. The card tells us to regard money in our lives as energy, as something live and volatile like gasoline. In some stages of life we need money to do things, to accomplish goals (setting up a home, buying a boat perhaps). It is an empowering tool At other times money becomes an end in itself and is destructive. It can be a dirty word. It can clog up and muddy your psyche. Freud perceived it as 'anal retentionsm' and the link between muck or excreta is seen through our language.

The card is like a coin that has two sides. Heads you win, tails you lose. Being deprived of it – real poverty – is appalling; all too often it kills our potential. Yet too much money can shut doors, not open them. People who are rich can be trapped in a money-world and lose their humanity. Money, too, is another form of psychological security. The reassurance that a wad of notes or a fat bank balance brings is like that of a child's comforter. Is the Money Card suggesting you are substituting money for love (like George Eliot's *Silas Marner* who lost his money but found a child)?

Money is part of our social world. On every street corner there are shops, and the exchange of goods for money is part of our social economy too. Going to the shops – whether it is to Saks or the local drugstore – makes up an important element is our lives. The Money Card highlights this and asks whether you are by temperament a spender or a squirreller.

The cards in a spread will help you see some of the ways money plays in your life. If it is nearby to the Voyage Card, maybe it is telling us to embark on a financial enterprise. Near the Beauty it could alert you to a valuable work of art. Next to the Warrior it could tell you to muster your courage to ask for a salary increase.

The card then advises you to treat money in your life as a dog that needs discipline and respect. It should not be over-pampered. If it runs loose it may bite someone. Be sure that money knows you are the master.

ASSOCIATIONS AND OPPOSITES

Salary and Income	Poverty
Windfall	The feeling of being poor relative to others
Your Daily Bread	The Jam
Hoarding	Money
	Being a money-holic or spendthrift
Accountants and Banks	Betting shops, gambling and casinos
Pension	Commerce
	Shopping

THOUGHT PROMPTS

❖ Can you remember the feeling of getting your first pocket money as a child?

❖ Can you think of people whose lives have been changed by a lot of money for the better or the worse?

❖ How much of your social life centres round shopping?

❖ Do you think people who use money as psychological security would be happier to spend it and find other satisfactions?

11

FRIENDSHIP

No cordial can the heart renew
Like laughter with a friend or two

It is as old as the hunting pack, as old as the group huddled round the fire when the night is resonant with fear. Friendship is fundamental to our happiness, and this card reminds us of the value of the circle of old friends and new.

The picture is of olden times like people from a storybook. They are a group of friends in a tavern, maybe they are in a seaport, and one is a sailor who has brought the parrot from exotic parts. They are telling each other stories and swapping gossip and supping a jar or two.

Of course there are levels of friendship. We can have a casual nodding acquaintance with people in the pub, or in the supermarket, or at work. But real friendship is something more. It means people we are relaxed with, with whom we can drop our masks.

One of the messages of the card is that friendship for most people needs hard work. Some people make friends easily and on a superficial level. Others are shy and find it hard to make the initial contact. In Jung's categories we are likely to incline to be either outgoing extroverts or reserved introverts. The former find friends come and go; the latter fewer but deeper relationships. Maybe some of the closest bonds are across the two categories where an outgoing person compensates for the unsociable nature of the other and vice versa, and where both benefit from a supportive trading relationship.

Friends are a compensation for what we ourselves lack and people make friends at times when they need support. When we are lonely in our first week of school or when we are working under a difficult boss, or are in times of pain or loss, these are times when the seeds of friendship are sown. Around a campfire or in a dormitory or in a hospital in a strange town, or on a holiday which does not live up to expectations, we will very often find the friends of a lifetime.

People who seek a common goal find friends as a by-product of their enterprise. The Three Musketeers, The Famous Five, and Robin Hood and his Merry Men will have all had much to reminisce about together. So if you seek new friendship, embark on a new venture!

The Friendship Card can remind us to support and strengthen and make contact with old friends by letter and phone, and by mending minor quarrels. Our friendships, like our clothes, must be kept in good repair. It can also prompt us to extend our social life and talk to a neighbour to whom we have just previously nodded. Friendship blossoms in parties. Could the card suggest you ask a few people round and sow some seeds?

The Friendship Card is about circles. Within it we all have roles: one is the organiser, one the listener, one the joker. Some circles can be too tight when they form barriers to the outside world. A clique that is exclusive, cemented by snobbery or sport or art or religion, can seem hostile to outsiders. Enmity can be generated in this way among people who fall out and people who seek to penetrate their clique. Cults and gangs are not products of true friendship, because they are defensive.

You need your place in the magic circle around the

camp fire. You need the shoulder to cry on and to have a good laugh. But the Friendship Card asks you to squeeze in an outsider to share the warmth.

ASSOCIATIONS AND OPPOSITES

Neighbours	
Circles	
Work friends	Gangs, cults, cliques
School friends	Loneliness
Conviviality	
Parties	Enmity
Dropping roles and masks	False Jollity
Gossip	
Rigid formality and Strict manners	
Talking	Indifference
Working at friendship	TV
Welcoming others	
Pets Pubs and Clubs	

THOUGHT PROMPTS

❖ Picture your first friend and how and when you met.
❖ Can you think of some unhealthy friendships among people you know?
❖ When did you last make a new friend? How and Why?
❖ Can you think of characters on TV or in books where friendship merges into either love or hatred?

12

FORTUNE

*Destiny calls you if you dare
To win the prize that's waiting there*

You maybe have a special destiny. It is more than being lucky in love or lucky in cards. It is more than your inheritance of genes or what someone will leave you in their will. You will find it. It will find you. That is the Fortune Card.

The picture shows a seeker of truth, an adventurer, a man, a woman, climbing a winding staircase in some dark tower. He or she cannot see it, but that which is sought is awaiting and the reward is abundant. Perhaps the seeker has a map and the clues have led to this mysterious place; the winding stairs means you cannot see what is ahead. The lamp he or she carries symbolises the search for truth. The treasure which we can see might be a hoard of pirate gold which can bring untold wealth, or the spiritual treasure symbolised in the Holy Chalice that we can see in the Union Card.

The message of the Fortune Card is to stay faithful to your own destiny. Destiny, your star, luck, fate, kismet... what do they mean? Psycards certainly does not suggest that everything in our lives is pre-ordained. Its belief is that we have control and choice over what matters. This is not incompatible with the idea that we have a special destiny. The card is pointing you up the winding stair to find your own unique path that ascends upwards to your higher self and your own inner development. It is telling you to have faith in yourself and its message is not to be down-hearted by negative thinking and criticism.

Today it is recognised that much of our fortune is written in our genes. So some of us have a propensity to longevity, others to disease. The way each of us handles and responds to these genetic challenges is unique to each individual. Your life divides into elements over which you can and cannot exert control. You can do little about your sex, your parents, your stature, your nationality. This card is about the interface of these two halves. Your fortune is how you accept or fight or transcend them, or work with your 'lot'.

The bells of Bow called a despondent Dick Whittington to turn again and become Lord Mayor of London. Florence Nightingale overcame the derision that a mere woman should become involved in the male business of war. Joan of Arc had her 'voices'. Socrates had his Guardian Angel. The Fortune Card is reminding us of what is special about us. So we should not listen too much to conventional wisdom and sceptical common sense, if we seek to discover what is 'in store' for us, as the treasure chest in the Card is showing.

The Card has some other implications. Some people are born lucky. It is called charm or magnetism or charisma. In love or in business or in war, we need to be aware if this indefinable gift is in our vicinity. Roman legionaries knew exactly which generals were lucky like Julius Caesar.

This too is very much the card for self-development. We cannot stand still. Growth and change can never be resisted. We need to move ahead emotionally and spiritually. The growth process is step by step and like the winding stair we cannot see the path in front. The finding of our true self and the fulfilment of our inner potential is the quest.

The Fortune Card can often best be seen by those cards that surround it. The Peace card may remind us to seek inner spiritual growth. The Sage may suggest you should seek some wise counsel of your own path. But it tells you that you have a destiny, and it is yours to find it.

ASSOCIATIONS AND OPPOSITES

Things in store for you	Believing you are victimised
Destiny	Being one of a herd
Luck	Self-doubt
Kismet	
Guardian Angel	
Personal Development	Negative thinking
Self-confidence	Criticism

THOUGHT PROMPTS

❖ Do you know people who deep inside themselves believe that have a special destiny? Do you think it might be true of yourself?

❖ Do you know people who are lucky in life? How do you explain it?

❖ Do you know people who have lost their path in life and then re-found it?

❖ Can you think of people in stories who followed their star in some way and it led them to fulfilment?

13

THE FATHER

You are his seed. So stand up high
Who sired you points you to the sky

Fathers are unfashionable these days. Luckily we still need them even after the moment of conception.

It is the first of the Psycard Archetype Cards which are the templates that shape our humanity. They are buried deep into our psyches and they recur in many different guises through our lives. We all have a biological father and as well a model of fatherhood with positive and negative qualities attached to it. The Father Card unravels for us some of the threads that make us what we are.

The picture shows a father teaching his son how to shoot a bow and arrow. He is giving guidance, pointing the boy into new directions. The arrows are perhaps related to the Skills Card. It is about teaching and tenderness and the transmission of techniques across the generations. It reminds us we are stewards of skills.

What are the qualities of an ideal father? He must protect his child from danger. He must provide sustenance for his child. He must have authority. He must love the mother. He must teach the child and love him or her. We all measure the real father against the ideal.

So the Father Card asks us to bring to mind our own real father and what he has or has not done for us. Our reactions are governed by our upbringing, our position in the family as siblings and our specific situation. We may have feelings of affection, admiration, humour or anger. It may raise thoughts about the nuclear family and how well has it worked in our case. But we need to know what we feel.

While mothering is always close to a child, fathering can be done at a distance. Good fathers can be away hunting moose or at sea or on oil rigs and still be fulfilling their fatherhood roles. The card should remind us never to forget the influence of the absent father.

There are other aspects of the Father Card. It is about morality and obedience and rebellion. For some 10,000 years – excepting us perhaps in the last 30 years in West – the world has lived in a largely patriarchal society. The father of the family, the tribe, the clan, the village elder, the squire upheld the rules of society. In Judaism, Christianity and Islam God is HE. He loves us but wants us to be good. He is at times forbidding and stern. He demands obedience. Sometimes He punishes.

'Sky' Fathers are fine but when they come down to earth there are problems and this card highlights it. It is flashing out a warning on Morality, the rules of our society. Maybe it is telling us, 'Don't be naughty'. More likely it is saying we are being dogmatic and moralistic. Are we punishing somebody – most likely the person nearest to us – ourselves?

Fathers breed rebels. Every authoritative society and family will foster dissidents. It is an age-old and beneficial pattern for conflict to exist between the generations. Where the Father is, a Child is looking to break loose.

The proximity of other cards with the Father Card will give a steer of its immediate relevance to us. The

Liberation Card may tell us of a someone seeking to break away. The Tower can indicate a domineering father.

Our fathers seeded us. They pass down to us gene treasures we have inherited. They build walls to protect our childhood. They teach us the rules to operate in society. They point us upwards to the sky. And in time we will break away from them.

ASSOCIATIONS AND OPPOSITES

Father as Head of the Family	
Father as Protector	
Father as Provider	
Father as Teacher	
Father as Father Christmas	Punishment
Morality	Immorality
Obedience	Rebellion
Father figures	Bosses
Priests	
The Next Generation	Flying the coop

THOUGHT PROMPTS

❖ Can you think of children who have suffered from weak fathering and others from an overbearing fathering?
❖ What is the first picture you have of your own father?
❖ Can you think of ways that single mothers can strengthen father images in children with as absent father? Should they do so?
❖ Can you think of father and son or father and daughter conflicts in stories?

14

THE MOTHER

Love and pain is her reward
She mothers best who breaks the cord

Your relationship with the first person you encountered will set the pattern of your life. Understand that and you will understand yourself. This is the message of the Mother Card.

It shows mother and children. Mother, son, daughter and baby are posed almost as in a Victorian photo. The shape of the chair may suggest the womb.

We are mammals programmed to receive mothering, and there is no surprise to have the archetype of the Mother ingrained in our psyches. Our happiness and characters are based on the strength of our relationship with our mother and the way we have grown out of it.

Motherliness is warmth and support; it is protection and the generosity of the good breast. It is feeding and home building and comfort and reassurance and the promise that you have a place in a hostile world. It is space to experiment and to make mistakes without being criticised. Men too can mother ideas and enterprises and the card alerts us to these nursing and caring qualities in either sex.

A bird with its fledglings, a she-bear with cubs defends her young with ferocity. Evolution has equipped us with a powerful mother instinct. So the Mother Card reminds us that we are faced with a formidable instinctual force that can wreck the best laid plans. Beware the combination of the Mother Card with the Destruction Card!

We learn from the earliest years, even from within the womb, the art of love and the process of socialisation. We do, of course, seek to monopolise her and the anguish of separation forces us into the painful growth of being separate identities. The card then alerts us to the earliest shaping of our personalities.

Family relationships generate tension between mother and son, and mother and daughter. Mother-son relationships are often about possessiveness and mothering can become the smothering of maleness in some boys. Mother-daughter problems can be caused by envy or because both parties see too much of themselves in the other.

The Mother Card warns us to watch out for possessiveness. Some mothers are 'emotional imperialists' (in Tarot the Empress can be the Mother Card equivalent); they seek to dominate and control the inner lives and feelings of their children. Good mothers know the right time to encourage their fledglings to try a spot of flying. The theme of clinging comes back at the end of the generation cycle when mothers seek support and nurture from their own daughters.

The Mother Archetype is linked with the fertility goddess who made the crops grow. Sometimes named Astarte, Isis or Demeter she was a powerful force in ancient times. The Virgin Mary has attracted to herself many of these rich associations and is an intercessor between man and God. The Christian Church is known as Mother Church which enfolds all believers to her skirts.

The Mother Card reminds us too of an important weapon that can be used for good or evil. It is the importance of food which is a function of motherhood. Food is love. We can show love through food. Apple pie is one outward sign of motherliness. Families are fostered by the family table. Food gives mothers power to control and ration, and to dispense love, to punish and deny it to some.

The Mother Card promises you warmth and abundance and the fecundity of nature. It reminds you of your upbringing and the process of growing away from your mother to find your own identity.

ASSOCIATIONS AND OPPOSITES

Nurturing	Smothering
Warmth	Possessiveness
Compassion	
Clinging on Fertility	Childlessness
Home Making	
Feeding	
The Generous Breast	Snow White's Step Mother
The Mother Goddess	The Moon Goddess
The Virgin Mary	
Mother Church	
Our Infancy and Upbringing	The Crone, the Witch

THOUGHT PROMPTS

- ❖ What in your experience causes mother-daughter conflicts?
- ❖ Does your experience tell you that men have a mothering instinct?
- ❖ Do some women lack a mothering instinct?
- ❖ Can you think of stories where mothers have a destructive influence on their children?

15

BIRTH

*Time is come. Triumphant through
Bursts the miracle of the New*

Might it be possible that you are pregnant? You, Sir, or you, Madam? The Birth card alerts us to that something is being born around you or maybe from inside you. A human life is one possibility. Or a plan to write a book or redesign the garden or patch up a quarrel or start a new political party. And remember when something is coming up to birth it takes quite a lot to stop it.

The Birth Card shows a new shoot taking root, dewy, vernal and triumphant. It is both fragile yet unstoppable.

This card is about creativity, and we have to start with the miracle of the birth of a child. It is easy to talk in clichés but the birth of a baby, a clear indisputable minute human being, with fingers and toes and a package of genes and a destiny of his or her own is seen by its parents quite rightly as a thing of wonder. The birth of every child shows ripples in the family, the community and the whole universe. It changes something; it displaces what was there before.

The most important thing about the Birth Card is to dismiss sentimentality. No blue and pink bootees, please. Birth means pain. Aside from the physical birth pangs, birth causes disruption to the status quo. To accommodate a new baby in a family threatens siblings and plays havoc with treasured routines and evokes jealously. King Herod who slaughtered the Innocents knew something. Babies are ruthless and insistent and get their way. They are dictators and abolish democracy.

The Birth Card tells us that around us things are in

gestation, and have acquired a momentum of their own. This truth extends beyond human birth. The creation of new elements in our psyches has its own forces and cannot be gainsaid. You can play with an idea or make some plans and still be in control, but once the birth process sets root, it grows like an embryo of its own accord. You are the carrier. Aborting the birth process is possible in many cases but, beware, nature will get its revenge.

Sometimes the card is telling us we are being midwives or fosterers of something new. We are not its mother or father but we are being asked to bring it about. The role of a midwife or facilitator is important. A producer facilitates the play or film while the author or director may conceive. Business and management and financial skills are needed to bring about an inspired brainchild.

Birth is usually a co-operative act. Around the cradle are benign or malignant godparents. When you see the Birth Card ask yourself who are in attendance.

There is another broader message. It says hope. In all our endeavours, we need the hope of things improving in order to motivate us to complete our tasks. Hope is the light at the end of the tunnel and this card promises that.

Babies need names. One of the ways to recognise Birth is the generation of names and identities. Some people and ideas can get reborn, re-branded, re-launched in the world. Maybe the Birth card is asking you to find some names for people and things in your inner and outer world.

The archetypal Birth is the Christmas story which implies with it the shadows of death. Myths cluster round the births of every nation. Rome was born when Romulus and Remus were suckled by a she-wolf. Birth brings with it wonders and you must expect it.

Rejoice and be prepared. The Birth Card is alerting us to something new in our life.

ASSOCIATIONS AND OPPOSITES

Gestation	Pain
Creation	Birth pains
A new idea taking root	Abortion
The Birth process	
Midwives	
Fairy – and real godparents	Wicked godparents
Embryos	Death
Hope	Despair
Spring	Autumn
Names and Identities	
Re-birth	
Birthdays	

THOUGHT PROMPTS

❖ When you were born what disruption ensued?
❖ What stories were told about your birth?
❖ Do you see yourself as a mother or a midwife to new plans, ideas and projects?
❖ In your experience what happens if you stop the birth process?
❖ What stories, news, or TV come up where the birth of a baby makes great changes in the world?

16

DEATH

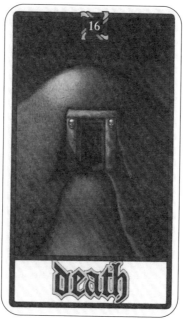

Don't fear this card…it seeks to send
This plea: 'I want to be your friend'

For some people this card may come as bad news. It tells you are going to die. Not for some time we hope, but one day all of us will die and this future event alters our lives now. Death means the end but it also means the start of something else. The presence of death is integral to our lives.

You may feel this is a frightening card, and Psycards stresses that when it turns up in a reading, it does not denote imminent death

The picture shows an ancient burial mound with a gateway to a dark tunnel. It is an Entrance not an Exit. The sky is grey, maybe early dawn. Two skulls are carved into the door pillars. Poppies carpet the grass either side of the pathway. The shape of the tomb is mysterious, the colours are muted browns and greys. The poppies are for remembrance, their colour for courage.

The Death Card has layers of meaning. Perhaps it is best to think of it as the fear of death. Look at a corpse: death itself is small and shrunk. The fear of death is huge with menace. Consider how we invent euphemism for death: 'passing away', or skirt around it with jokes like 'kick the bucket'. Death is taboo and we avert our eyes like those Victorians who clothed piano legs for fear that they would incite them to lewdness. One of the messages of the card is that we need to confront our fears and that if we can face the fear of death we can face anything.

The card is not only about physical death. Often it says the end of something. It may be telling you that a relationship has come to an end, or you should break a habit, or that your stay in that home is over, or that your job is a dead end.

The picture shows a gateway. Birth and death are locked in a recurrent cycle where winter gives way to spring. On a common-sense basis nothing can be born without death making space for it. It is especially true for the economy of our psyches. We can't start something new until we say goodbye to something old.

It seems that all human beings were fixated by death whereas animals are not. The earliest peoples made it sacred, and sought to honour their ancestors. All religions are in a sense a way out of dying. The Egyptians' monumental art is designed to say death has no dominion. Freud tells us all civilisation is a way of facing up to its unspeakable power.

The Psycards Death Card asks us at some times to face the prospect of our own deaths. If we believe in life after death – which most civilised people for 6000 years have believed – we still find it awesome.

Today it reminds us too of old age. If death is a gateway or an embarkation point for another shore, our old age had to be a preparation for a journey. We are perhaps not allowed to collect our bus pass and relax. We have work to do. One of the messages of this card is that we can only make sense of the last quarter of our lives and enjoy them by making terms with death.

The card reminds us that the death of a loved one needs a period of grieving or bereavement. The healing process has to come to terms with death and this card is asking us to be alert to it in others as well as ourselves.

Death is natural. It has its own times and suicide and euthanasia are an affront to it.

The cards that adjoin the Death Card may tell us more. The Tower Card may remind our Ego has to die if other parts live. The Peace card can point us to higher spiritual levels. But its message for you is clear. Something in your life is ending or needs to end.

ASSOCIATIONS AND OPPOSITES

Finality,	
A dead end	Gateways
The end of a phase of our lives	
	Resurrection
	A journey, a port
The fear of death	
The after world	The taboo of death
Courage	Funerals, burials
Peace and reconciliation	Bereavement
The Spirits of the Dead	Old age
Tombs	
Natural death	Violent death

THOUGHT PROMPTS

❖ Have you ever seen a dead body? In what ways in your own experience does the death of a relationship bring forth a new life?

❖ Is talking and thinking about death unhealthy and morbid? Or is it better to just take the dying as for granted and not make too much fuss?

17

THE LIBIDO

The joy of life this potent juice
Is never yours for private use

L ibido is the Latin word for pleasure. Freud used it as the primal sexual that drives us all. And the Libido Card stands for this basic element in our lives.

The card depicts the Garden of Eden in bright morning light. A little stream bubbles down from a rock. Two peacocks flaunt themselves, a brilliant snake suns itself in the grass. The snake, the garden, the unashamed exuberance, the flushing water has sexual symbolism but the message is joy and innocence.

The story of the card is that we are built for joy and happiness and we can find it. We seek pleasure; we shun pain. It is natural and right. The first satisfactions of a baby – suckling and warmth – are the spring that feeds the river that runs through our lives. Think of pleasure as energy to fuel us in the way a gasoline fuels a car. We cannot achieve any of our goals without the tigers in our tank. This primal energy source is closely linked to our sexual nature, though it can be and needs to be channelled, sublimated, and redirected.

So the Libido Card calls us to remember our own nature and trust in it. It tells us to go and play. It points us to fulfil ourselves in both our romantic and sexual aspects. And it says that this force should spill itself into other departments of our lives. You can't do your work properly if you don't enjoy it. The same is true of our friends, our bodies and our leisure activities. If you do any of these things joylessly you will do them badly. In its wider sense love does make the world go round.

The Libido Card asks us to be more demanding

about sex in our lives and certainly does not give us a licence to do what we want. Its command is joy, not self-indulgence and it knows too much coupling can be joyless. It warns us against liaisons where dominance or ownership is a strong ingredient. Its patron saints are Blake and D.H. Lawrence, proponents of a sort of pure fierce Puritan morality. We are being gently warned to expect disapproval and negative criticism. There is always a battle between morality and conventions and narrow-mindedness on one side and between spontaneity and freedom. This card tells you to trust your instincts. Blake says 'Damn braces, bless relaxes'. He warns us against nurturing unfulfilled desires.

Yet the Libido card is ambivalent. If we think of it as a potent fuel, it alerts us to its dangers. Because, if it spills out in certain situations, it is disruptive. Some hundred thousand novels must have been written about how romantic love and sexual passion destroys, marriages, societies or thrones. Troy burned because of the libido of Helen and Paris.

To suppress it is dangerous too. If you force your natural desires down inside yourself there is a danger they will surface in other more malignant guises. You can't just wish away an energy force.

There are two ways to handle it: channel it and sublimate. Society and its institutions exist to tame our primal urges. Raw physical energy can be converted to sports, which are a sublimation of violence. Sexual energies flow into the bounds of marriages and stable relationships. Play energies turn to art. Our whole culture is energised by the libido.

The cards that adjoin the Libido Card can tell us into which aspects of our life this primal energy seeks to flow. (The Union Card may suggest a wedding. The Prison Card suggests your energies are dammed.)

The little mountain stream depicted in the card seeks to turn itself into a mighty river – if you can but channel it.

ASSOCIATIONS AND OPPOSITES

Sexual Drive	Marriage
Natural Instinct	Sublimation
Spontaneity Art,	Religion
Freedom	Disapproval
Desire, Joy	Social criticism
The life force	Destructive Violence
Energy	Rigid morality
Creativity	Destruction
The Pleasure Principle	The Death Wish
Playfulness	Narrow disciplines

THOUGHT PROMPTS

❖ In your experience is sex made more pleasurable if it has an element of being illicit?

❖ Do you know of people whose sex drives have been successfully channelled into non-sexual activities?

❖ How can you find ways to introduce creative play into your work, or your life?

❖ Can you think of personalities whose lives show a strong 'libido' element running through them?

18

DESTRUCTION

Now all we loved is lost. And Hate
Clamours angry at the gate

The Destruction Card asks you to face the collapse of what you most value. It asks you to be aware of the destructive instincts in yourself and in some of the people around you.

The picture depicts a town being put to sack in some medieval battle. The castle defending the town is burning. The church will fall. The peaceful monks are being slaughtered. Civilisation is falling to the barbarians. Women are tied to the stake. Is it futile vandalism or maybe the result of some ideology or religious dispute?

War, vandalism, wanton and futile destruction are unfortunately a part of human nature which does not change. This force is embodied in Hindu mythology in the form of the Goddess Kali who in one of her aspects devastates all around. The depiction of fire in the picture is instrumental. Fire destroys but it can be tamed and it can purify.

Earthquakes, massacre, war, natural disaster, the breakdown of society are items on the media and we devoutly pray that they will not stray into our everyday world. What then does the Destruction Card tell us? There are in the same way disasters in the personal sphere that happen to ourselves and others. Financial break-ups, breakdowns, the collapse of marriage you've struggled to maintain, sudden redundancy, the awareness of a serious illness, these have a seismic personal shock that make us wonder how we can continue. In all cases it is the opposite of all we've been building. We're cast in the dark, thrust down to the bottom of the snakes and ladders game at an unfair roll of the dice.

The Destruction Card reminds us not only of an Act of God, or an accident on the global motorway. Destructive forces – hatred – come from within the human heart. Some people want to pull things down: to kick over the child's pile of bricks, undermine someone's self-confidence and crush hope. We can be at the receiving end of crime and bullying and we know how child abuse and rape blights lives. We harbour destructive urges in ourselves and this card seeks to alert us to them.

One of the strongest messages of the Destruction Card is to look inside yourself. Are you destroying yourself? Addiction is one way; so is a corrosive self-hatred that can lead to the annihilation of the personality. Each one of us is invaluable, a storehouse of treasures built up over time. The card is warning us too of the destruction of the past, our own and our communal past. Our sense of identity depends on our history.

What consolation can the card offer? Scant. It says life goes on.. Out of the fire new growth emerges, just as when the farmer burns the stubble to produce the green shoots of spring, just as when the great fire of London cleared the space for St Paul's Cathedral to be built.

All things fall and are built again
And those that build them again are gay.
(W.B.Yeats).

The card points us to spiritual values, a permanent world 'where moth and rust cannot decay.' The Peace Card, if it falls nearby, reinforces this. The Warrior Card is relevant too because when Destruction looms we need outside intervention: a knight to rescue the damsel in distress.

Your treasure is threatened. Heed well the alarm bells that the Destruction Card rings.

ASSOCIATIONS AND OPPOSITES

Collapse of hopes	Rebuilding
Disaster out of your control	Seeking spiritual help
Wanton cruelty, crime	Seeking support and help
War	Peace
Life-shattering experiences	An explosive temper
Killing growth	Malevolence
A period of troubles	Keeping going
Barbarism	Civilisation
Madness	Sanity
Destructive fire	Purifying fire

THOUGHT PROMPTS

❖ In your own experience have you suffered a period when events destroyed your life? In what ways did you take control?

❖ In smaller ways can you think of malevolent and destructive urges in other people? How can you control them?

❖ In your experience how can people recover from 'destruction'?

❖ What examples can you find in books or stories from people suffering from destructive forces within themselves?

19

PEACE

*You'll find peace somewhere apart
To grow a garden in your heart*

Peace be with you, says this card. It stands for two important things in our life. One is our need for everyday tranquillity from the stress and strife around us. The other is spiritual growth.

The picture is of a great stained glass window, flooded with light which shines into the cool interior of a pillared cathedral. The window is a mandala, the Tibetan pattern which denotes one-ness, and the light beam is integrated in a single shaft. The colours are delicate and golden.

One of the messages of the Peace Card is that peace is not escapism or running away or rejection of the world and its problems. Peace is strength. Just as the massive architecture of the cathedral enfolds its inner sanctity, so inner peace needs outer strength and discipline. Peace is more than an absence of war or a temporary surcease of the warring factors within our souls.

Spiritual growth comes from a reconciliation of different elements. It means coming to terms with guilt and shame and what religious people call sin. With the decline of organised religion in the West many individuals pursue their own paths following Christian, Buddhist, Hindu or Sufi masters. But a religious tradition provides the discipline for the individual to find his or her own path to God. An awareness of a spiritual dimension comes to other people at different ages. Very often age or the awareness of death points people to eternal values, as the accoutrements of everyday life lose their attraction. Not all people have a spiritual gift or a hunger for the spirit. Many good people do not have it. But the Peace Card may be telling you that you should develop this part of your nature.

Peace is a gift from on high. We cannot manufacture it for ourselves but it is given to us if our egos are humbled and we follow certain disciplines. Prayer is one and, closely linked to it, is meditation.

Some people have the misapprehension that meditation or yoga is exclusively a religious path or an excuse to drop out. Meditation is a term for the altered states of consciousness which are controlled by exercises and sometimes helped by picture or speech patterns. Whatever process is used, if it is practised regularly it can diminish stress, provide mental control, encourage psychic awakening and permit peace to enter the soul.

There is a less exalted way to look at the Peace Card, which is important. It tells us that everyday in some circumstances for a week or so we need to withdraw from the hurly burly of living to a peace of inner relaxation physically and mentally. We are being told to re-charge our batteries. Sunday is the day of the Peace Card. It needs a commitment and a discipline. The card also reminds us to seek solace on occasions in those very precious places which have a special meaning to us. It may be a place from our childhood or from a holiday. As the poet Yeats said of the Isle of Innisfree,

'And I shall have some peace there,

 For peace come dropping slow'

The Peace Card has another message for us. It tells us to make peace in our own lives. Reconciliation and ending quarrels, bridge-building between two warring parties is a high moral calling. It also brings psychic peace.

What do you seek in life? Wealth, intelligence, beauty, success? Without peace of mind none of these are worth anything. The Peace Card points us to this truth.

ASSOCIATIONS AND OPPOSITES

Tranquillity	Stress
Relaxation	
Overcoming guilt	
Meditation	
Spiritual growth	Materialism
Mystical paths	
Religious disciplines	The rampant ego
A haven	
Eternal values	
Everyday worries	
Reconciliation	Quarrel
Monasteries, retreat	

THOUGHT PROMPTS

❖ Where do you find periods of inner relaxation in your life?

❖ Do you know people who demonstrate a quality of peace of mind?

❖ In your experience does religion help people find peace of mind?

❖ Who do you know in TV or stories who you'd associate with the Peace Card?

20

THE SUN

Fortunate you. Its kindly ray
Prospers well your fate today

The Sun shines on you. It promises success. It melts away opposition, But it has a shadow side. The sun is the first of the Symbols and one of those basic cards that have a rich cluster of associations around them.

The card depicts a benign sun under which the ripe corn stands high, ready to be cut in sheaves, and in the harvest festival the children dance around the maypole. The colours are summer-y with bright blues, yellows and orange.

The sun is the dominant force in our planet. People from the earliest time knew it powered the abundance of nature, and set the pace for the seasons and governed the rhythms under which they operated. It stands then and now for warmth, clarity, reason and fulfilment.

The Sun Card, like the Now Card (which relates to specific courses of action you are considering) tells us to make hay while the sun shines, that there are psychological times that are opportune for us, and that we should enjoy happiness. In the past we have sowed well; now we can reap the fruits.

The Sun has always been seen as a god – by the Greeks, a chariot driven by Apollo, or a fierce creative force to be appeased by human sacrifice by the Aztecs and Incas. You cannot look direct at the midday sun, and its nature is you cannot really argue with it, and this points us to some of the things that the card is saying to us.

It has always been seen as a potent male force whereas the earth and the moon are seen as female. So

it stands for many of the assertive masculine characteristics – which can of course be manifested in either sex.
The sun is bossy. It lays down the rules. The card is then
alerting us to certain people in our lives and certain
elements in ourselves. 'Sun' people like order and
control. They see everything as clear and obvious, cut
and dried, clear as daylight. They believe in logic and
common-sense, as defined by them. They seek direct
solutions. They are optimists – after all the sun is
shining now and it will again tomorrow.

They are disposed to classic values in art. they are
extroverts directed to the outside world and are cheerful
and confident, and indeed people cluster in admiration
around them like satellites. Everything is out in the
open. Everything is ordered and measured. When we
come to the Moon card how pronounced the polarities
are!

Maybe we are sun people ourselves. Maybe not. But
the card is positive. It radiates generosity. It casts its
benign countenance on the other cards it sits next to.
(The Sun and the Voyage Card virtually tells you to
pack your passport and sunglasses!) Like the Now Card
it tells us to seize the hour and it boosts our confidence.

But there are warnings too. The sun has a shadow
side. Its assertive light generates its own darkness which
breeds negativity and rebellion. It can be pitiless.
Exposure to the Sun can have the psychological
equivalent of severe sunburn. It shrivels tender growth
and can create a desert round it. It can kill, too, by
encouraging over confidence. Icarus was a mythological

Greek aviator who flew too near the sun which melted the wax that glued his wings and plunged him to death.

Enjoy the sun card. Bask in its rays, Remember all the time that the sun in its daily course rises and sets. So ask yourself what hour it is in your psychic sky.

ASSOCIATIONS AND OPPOSITES

Warmth	The Moon
Generosity	
Success	Withering heat
Common sense	
Dominance	Denying other logics
Clarity	
Bossiness	The obvious answer
Superficiality	
Order	
The Shadow Control	
Energy	
Extroversion	
Maleness	
Classic Values	

THOUGHT PROMPTS

❖ Do you believe you have cycles in your life when the sun element is dominant?
❖ Do you know people who live in the shadow of someone else's sun?
❖ Do you know women who have strong sun propensities?
❖ Which members of your family and friends do you associate with this card?

21

THE MOON

Intuition's silver light
Can make the path before you bright

The lesser light of the moon invites us into territory where the sun cannot reach: the realms of intuition and imagination. The Moon Card tells us to be swayed by what emerges from your unconscious and remember there is a feminine logic as well as a male logic.

In the picture the full moon queens it over the ocean, and tempts a sea creature from the depths. The serene blues and greens reinforces the mystery. The crab may have links with the astrological sign, or maybe it's because it doesn't move directly to its goal, but crab-wise.

'Sun' and 'Moon' are in balance to each other, polarised dualities. Male and female, day and night, extrovert and introvert, classic and romantic, art and science, reason and imagination, water and earth, yin and yang, conscious and unconscious, head and heart all work together in opposites. We can see them in conflict or as partners in a great cosmic dance to divine music. Its rhythms govern everything we do. We need to see whether we are moon or sun people.

Intuition means applying an alternative route to a problem. The sun's goes direct, straight, obvious, on the surface. The moon from her depths finds a better way that reflects the sensitivities of the people involved, because most problems focus on people. Some of us have strong intuitions and they can be fostered and encouraged. It really means listening to oneself. Linked to it are psychic gifts. We all accept that some people have musical gifts. Some people have enhanced awareness of the psychic world and can pick up sonar echoes from the depths.

In Psycards the Moon Card represents the unconscious part of ourselves. On a simplified Freudian model the unconscious is a dark cellar into which forbidden things get put. They climb up to disturb us up the cellar steps (the sub-conscious). With Jung the unconscious is an ocean upon which our brave little boat (the ego) sails. The subconscious is the beach where conscious and unconscious meet. Psycards follows Jung.

Out of our depths come dreams. We can occasionally fish up some precious creature or object from our sleep in the morning. Dreams, of course, are one way for the unconscious to talk to us. The Moon Card reminds us to look again at some recent dreams we have had.

Another message is to go back to our imaginations. The Sun is real. The moon allows us half light where fantasies can play. Everything starts in the mind and then comes out to the everyday world. Grow seeds in the seed beds of the heart and plant them out in full sun in your garden.

The feminine side, the alternative side needs its equal sway. King and Queen, Sun and Moon are both enthroned within us, whatever gender we are. The Moon stands for alternative solutions, be it alternative politics, art or medicine. Maybe the Moon is subversive and is seen as anti-social. The Romantic movement rebelled against society in the name of individualism and the moon sailed strong in the minds of artists, poets and musicians of the time. When the sun is extrovert, the moon shines brightest in the inner world of the introvert.

There is of course a negative side to the moon: moodiness, fickleness and even madness. Whereas the sun is a round triumphant disc, the waxing and waning of the moon from crescent to full reminds us of inconstancy..

Look at her image on the card or on a fine night when she sails majestically through the clouds. Her influence is on you.

ASSOCIATIONS AND OPPOSITES

Intuition	
Imagination	
Moodiness	
The Unconscious	
Inconstancy	
Feminine logic	The Sun's values
Introversion	Logic
Fantasy	Male dominance
Dream	Science
The Individual	
Psychic gifts	

THOUGHT PROMPTS

❖ Do you think you can alternate sun thinking with moon thinking?
❖ Are you governed more by intuition than by logic?
❖ Do you find your dreams meaningful?
❖ What person of your acquaintance would you most associate with the Moon card?

22

THE STARS

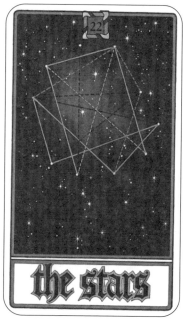

the stars

What is above is found below
Go where Heaven bids you go

'Reach up,' says the Star Card, 'Set your sights higher.'

It pictures the immensity of the night sky exploding and pulsing soundlessly with energies governed by laws we can only half guess at. Over it we can see patterns that shape ourselves and our world.

Our distant forefathers knew that sun and moon affected their lives and their agriculture but it was one of the marks of the first civilisations to understand the rhythms of the constellations which gave us time measurement and initiated both astronomy and astrology. Today there is a divergence between these two which is comparatively recent. Yet they are both about the ultimate questions: where did we come from? where are we going to?

The card tells us what we do on earth is linked to what is in the heavens and the implication for us is threefold. The card is about destiny and can reinforce the Fortune Card. Some people have a marked destiny and they know they must follow their star. This does not imply that our lives are pre-destined. Most astrologers allow us a large element of free will. Our stars incline or pre-dispose at birth. Along with our genes and our social backgrounds we have characters. We are given certain cards to play. But it is up to us to play them. So the message of the card is to be ambitious for yourself. You may have a gift – artistic talent or leadership maybe – that is star-stuff. You may be made for better things in your career or your personal life. Are you being too small-minded about your potential?

Lastly the card is suggesting we find another perspective to our lives. In many of the situations we find ourselves in we need to distance ourselves from the everyday. Step back, says the Star Card, you are too close to see things clearly. Our concerns are painful, and we can sometimes ease the pain by seeing them in another context. What looms as life-shattering today will feel different next week and next year. The card reminds us of what our grandfathers might have described as the 'eternal verities'.

This card then tells you 'Look, look up at the Stars.' Do not be fazed by short-term nuisances. They are of little account in the aeons of star time. For you – for all of us the stars foretell exciting news We have a role in the great drama of the starry universe.

ASSOCIATIONS AND OPPOSITES

Truth	False Illusions
Eternity	Trivia
Science	Thinking you are nothing
Destiny	
Your potential	Thinking Small
Guidance	Being earth-bound
Awe	Humility
Ambition	
Aspiration	
The Divine	

THOUGHT PROMPTS

❖ Do you believe you have a special destiny? Do you know people who believe they have?

❖ Do you know people who should raise their sights in order to fulfil their potential?

❖ Is there a danger in having your head in the clouds and falling on the pavement?

❖ Which person in a story or on TV would you most associate the Star Card with?

23

THE TREE

Abundant foliage on high
Is fed by roots that hidden lie

'I was born thousands of years before you were born. I will be there thousands of years after you have died. I will protect you. I will help you grow.'

This is the message that the Tree carries.

The card depicts a tree in a symbolic shape with the leaves balanced by the roots. Seasons come and go but the tree gives forth its leaves each spring. Its fruits nurture us. When the storm winds blow it has the resilience to cope with the stresses. The colours are perhaps a vibrant red for energy. The tree has been pruned – a fact that has a relevance for us.

Like us the tree has roots in the earth and aspires to the sky. The tree symbol occurs throughout our religion, culture and literature and art. Eve plucked the apple from the Tree of Knowledge in the Garden of Eden. The mystical Kabbala celebrated it. It is the Bo Tree under which Buddha sat, the tree with the Golden Bough from which ancient people hung sacrifices to appease the local gods and, of course, the cross of Christ.

The Tree Card promises us growth. It encourages us to fulfil a potential psychologically and spiritually, Growth comes from the balance between roots and branches; health and happiness need to be fed from roots deep within the unconscious and our past, and our energies flow in an integrated system. Gardeners know that trees are responsive and their growth can be shaped. So too our inner trees need to be pruned. If we lop branches here we can encourage growth elsewhere.

If one relationship or aspect of our life is cut off there is a compensation. The Tree Card is reminding us of the truth about the economics of psychic energy.

It tells us too we cannot grow without protection. When the storms are blowing we seek the cover the Tree can give us. (Trees have always been as a refuge. Charles II hid away in an oak tree from his pursuers. Robin Hood fled to the Greenwood). For us our families are where we first seek for protection.

Our family tree goes back generation by generation to the first men; we are the latest green leaves. Today we often refer to the nuclear family and neglect the wider extended family. Our kith and kin, grandparents, cousins, and all can be valuable for us when the storms are blowing.

The tree stands also for society and the political state we live in. However atomised socially, we are not free-standing individuals. Our attitudes, habits, language, and laws are the creation of a long process of history. We are living history, and no more free than an oak leaf to turn into a beech leaf.

So the message of the Tree Card is that we are not loners and our growth needs to be earthed into our society. As individuals we need the support, and protection of organisations, be they clubs, associations, the religious group, the company we work for, the local authority, and the Government. They are all trees in the forest and we are birds seeking nurture and protection in their branches.

There is another message in the Tree Card that is

urgent for everyone on the planet. It stands for our environment. The world's ecosystem is a whole. Our weather and our fertility is affected by the Brazilian rain forest. The creeping desertification in Africa, the burning of fossil fuels (dead forests) causes global warming. If the world tree is going to provide nests for future generations, we will all have to think green.

Plant the Tree Card in your heart.

ASSOCIATIONS AND OPPOSITES

Natural processes	
Roots	
Ancestry	
Protection	Exposure
Society	
Pruning shears	The axe
The environment	Deforestation
Organic growth	Forced growth
The family	
Institutions	
The long term	Short term answers
Patience	Impatience

THOUGHT PROMPTS

❖ In what way can you tell that someone has deep roots and someone else has shallow roots?

❖ In your own life has psychological growth come from inside or from outside influences?

❖ Can you think of examples where 'pruning' one part of your life encourages growth in another part?

❖ Do you think that pride in your family is a source of strength?

24

THE SCALES

*Natural justice governs you
She'll only give you what you're due*

There's the law of judges and policemen, the law of supply and demand, the Darwinian laws of the jungle. And the law of the Psyche. It is what is inscribed above the oracle at Delphi: 'Nothing too much'. Its first commandment is 'Thou shalt not go to extremes'. Balance is what is represented by the Scales Card.

The card depicts a pair of scales of justice hanging upon a tree abundant with fruit, which tumbles into the weighing pans. The Scales are the scales of natural justice and the fruit represents the gifts of life.

Greek philosophers pictured our psychology as a charioteer trying to control and balance three spirited horses. Freud saw us as composed of three elements: the drives from the unconscious (the id), the ego and the superego that sits in cantankerous judgement over us. We are told we are complex beings in an interdependent system. Managing the pressures, reconciling, harmonising and balancing them is the secret of our happiness.

There are always apparent conflicts: between work and leisure, family and friends, body, mind and soul, conscious and unconscious, optimism and pessimism, and whatever. It is up to us to find equilibrium between them. If we let the scales tilt too far one way, we have to correct them. Like a skater on the ice, we can only advance by balance.

Don't push it … compromise … a delicate touch on the tiller … exert a compensating pressure, these are the messages of the Scales Card. But it is very definitely not to pronounce judgements. Justice is the business of God and law courts and it is poison for us mortals. Judging shuts the prison doors on the psyche. Destructive criticism and prejudice can blight lives, and a burning feeling of injustice can corrode them. The trouble is that a 'puritan' conscience all too often imposes harsh standards on ourselves. The Scales Card pleads us to be kind.

(As the psyche, so the body. Your bathroom scales will echo the same message as the Scales Card. A balanced lifestyle will result in weight loss more effectively than any crash diet.)

The card raises the question of 'fairness'. It's unfair that he got that job, that she's got two cars, they have more holiday, or whatever. And it is unfair because, of course, life is unfair. The justice we get from judges and magistrates and policemen is fine. But we feel it is no substitute for 'real' justice, which will allot rewards and punishment according to our 'real' deserts. We hope there is justice which in time make things right in societies and individuals. All we can do is observe these natural laws in our lives and be patient for them to operate.

The Scales then are perhaps not blind. They tell us that prudence and moderation are not stuffy Victorian values. They are vital to help us handle our turbulent lives and they offer the apples of abundance to those who follow the commandment so the psyche.

ASSOCIATIONS AND OPPOSITES

Natural Justice	
Balance	Rigidity
Fairness	Unfairness
Prudence	Burning grievances
Moderation	Extremism
Generosity	The Rule Book
Forgiveness	Harsh Judgements
The Law	Legalism
Tolerance	

THOUGHT PROMPTS

❖ Do you know people whose life has been blighted by a burning feeling of grievance?

❖ Do you do yourself an injustice when your emotions are clouded by self-anger?

❖ Do you think you have been treated fairly or unfairly by life?

❖ Is it possible to learn psychological balance or is it something you are born with?

25

THE TOWER

Strong and proud above it all,
Will your looming fortress fall?

Are you strong and proud? Can anyone penetrate the fortification you've built? Are you riding for a fall? The Tower Card asks some of these questions.

A castle tower stands on a hill. Maybe an ogre lives there who dominates the surrounding countryside and makes extortionate demands on the peasantry. Or maybe it's a lonely princess. Maybe the castle is empty.

The Tower Card stands for the Ego. The Ego is Latin for 'I', the part in each of us who is 'managing director' of the different departments that make up the whole person. The Ego is liable to be a bit 'bossy', having to handle hungers, urges, instincts, and desires on one side (the 'id'), and the criticism of the superego (or our conscience, as it is traditionally called) on the other side. The Ego will put up defences, developing perhaps an outward personality that is a 'front' and sometimes does not reflect the sensitive soul within..

It is easy to regard the Tower Card as a negative card, which is unfair. In the Dark Ages when marauder Vikings surged in to rape, steal and destroy, the whole village rushed to safety to the local strong-point. The height of the tower enables them to see danger from afar. A strong personality is needed in troubled times to provide leadership and act as a rallying point. In day to day life we have to assert ourselves in social situations if we are to contribute our best. In a male environment the Tower Card calls on women to develop and practise assertiveness. (Towers, of course, do have phallic associations.) Confidence in ourselves is a necessary ingredient to functioning effectively.

In Tarot the Tower Card may often foretell disaster; lightning bolts bring down the battlements along with our illusions. In Psycards there are no inevitable consequences, and the Tower Card celebrates the need for self confidence.

But – and there is a but – very often confidence turns into something else: a closed mind, arrogance, pride, and a domineering and bullying attitude. All of these are warning signs for us.

Towers are static; if the village relocates they become inhabited only by the owls. Is there a message for some people who have built their personality around some past event and cannot develop out of it?

Towers, too, become fortresses or prisons. What looked like a secure job or a successful marriage can become a prison. The Tower Card also can indicate we are trapped inside ourselves, lonely and not able to communicate with people around us.

Human beings are never content with a good thing. No child can resist building their pile of bricks until they fall. The Bible told us of an early people who built the Tower of Babel so high that it invited divine anger. The Tower Card warns us of this human frailty and that pride wreaks its own destruction.

The Tower Card can stand too for the preservation of eternal values in a time which despises them – the last refuge of civilisation amid encroaching barbarism. Yeats declared the tower as one of his symbols,

A Storm-beaten old watch tower
A blind hermit rings the hour.

We all need to build defences for ourselves and your ego is your strength and protection. But take care you do not become walled inside it.

ASSOCIATIONS AND OPPOSITES

Strength	
Self-confidence	
The Ego	Bullying
	Dominance
Assertiveness	Arrogance
Pride	
	Refusal to listen
	Loneliness
Survival	Lack of communication skills
Traditional values	
Aristocracy	
A refuge	

THOUGHT PROMPTS

- ❖ Do you think that 'towers' are more likely to be men than women?
- ❖ Do you know people whose ego is so well protected that communication is difficult?
- ❖ How does self-confidence merge into cockiness?
- ❖ Is there any difference between pride and arrogance?
- ❖ What person you know most represents the Tower?

26

THE WHEEL

the wheel

*Go with its flow. Never be caught
Under the wheels of the juggernaut.*

What's the time? The clocks, the TV schedules, the train timetables tell you one thing. Maybe your heart is telling you another time. The Wheel Card warns us not to be trapped on a tiny wheel of time like a hamster in a cage but to watch and listen to the great cycles that govern us.

The card shows a mill wheel, turned by a busy stream. In the foreground the current has been slowed by the reeds. A brick wall into which the wheel is set seems forbidding, but we cannot forget that on the other side the wheel is grinding the corn to make the flour to bake the bread to feed the town.

Life goes on. Birth copulation and death…Monday follows Sunday…Autumn succeeds the Summer. Does nothing happen? The Wheel Card tells us it does, and that there is (as TS Eliot says) 'a time older than the time of the chronometers, older than time counted by anxious worried women, lying awake calculating the future'.

Human beings have cycles and wheels built into the architecture of their minds. The cyclical pattern of the seasons provided our ancestors with their livelihood and the movement of the stars their philosophy. The cycle of the generations, menstrual cycles, mood cycles, the business cycles that govern the economy, the electoral cycles that dictate our democracies… they all provide the rhythms that make up our world.

The Wheel Card seeks to remind us to understand our own cycles and rhythms. Planting seeds in the

Autumn will usually be unproductive, so too initiating a relationship or starting a business will only be fruitful when you are ready for it. We all have patterns – or biorhythms – and we need to understand them in order to take advantage of them. Many of us have mood swings related to the seasons. Christmas can strike deep gloom in some of us. Manic-depressive cycles occur in ordinary people as well as the more disturbed. Our bodies are affected by hormonal processes we only partially understand. Sensitivity to the psychic clocks of ourselves and others is vital.

There is another way this card is instructive. It asks us to trust, not just ourselves, but the tide of events or, one might say, the Universe. There is a stream of time that started with perhaps the Big Bang. We and the Milky Way are drifting on it and time only knows where it is going. We can be at peace with it. In Hebrew the turning of the wheel meant reincarnation which was central to the Kabbala which taught that the soul was recycled. Life then is an energy flow and death is nothing. It is the same in Buddhist philosophies where only the acceptance of the wheel, the eternal flux, gives us tranquillity and enlightenment.

Maybe this provides consolation with the feeling that our own lives are getting nowhere, that we are drifting , and are becalmed in the reeds in the picture. Sometime we see ourselves as broken on the wheel, victims crushed by the turn of events. Here the Wheel Card gives us consolation. Wheels turn. Things come round again to make things happen for us. Getting up, going to work, the daily grind may seem futile. But the energy flows in the world around us and within us is going to rescue us. The message is be of good cheer and be patient.

Circles and wheels are part of us. So are straight lines. Our ancestors used wheels to accomplish their goals, to carry their chariots to victory, to weave their cloth and make their pots. We can use wheels too to take us places.

ASSOCIATIONS AND OPPOSITES

Psychological Time	Digital clock
Time Cycles	
Rhythms	
The right opportunity	
Trust in time	Being hassled and hustled
Reincarnation	
Confidence in energy flows	
Continuity	
Repetition	Disruption
What goes up goes down	
Circles	Straight Lines, arrows

THOUGHT PROMPTS

❖ Do you have psychological cycles and are you able to moderate their effects on you?

❖ Are you depressed at the feeling of drifting or can you trust the stream of time to carry you ?

❖ Do you know people who accomplish their goals by circles rather than straight lines?

❖ Do you know people who are obsessed about clock-time, but blind to psychological time?

27

THE BEAUTY

*Powerful is she who has the art
To win a man and hold his heart*

Maybe she is you, maybe your beloved, maybe a rival, maybe a bitch. The Beauty Card tells us romantic love is in the air. It is the first of the Psycard Characters who will feature in our life story.

The picture shows a woman in a garden, finely apparelled. She looks mysterious and we can glimpse her expression reflected in the diamond panes of a window of the great house. Is she waiting for someone? Her beloved? Someone else's husband? Is she being spied on by jealous eyes? What is her secret?

She's Eve, Aphrodite, the Goddess of Love, Helen of Troy, Dante's Beatrice and the heroine of 100,000 paperbacks, and sometimes even the Virgin Mary. The Beauty Card stands for romantic love and for sexual attraction. She is the great love in someone's life.

Love is the most important thing in our lives. It does not come in neat compartments. It shifts its focus and we cannot control it. What we love we find beautiful and beauty itself can be dangerous.

Helen of Troy went off with another man in Homer's story. The results were a cruel war of ten years and the fall of a proud kingdom. Love builds dynasties and families and destroys them. Marriages and relationships are the shells in which love comes to dwell. It makes them and it can break them.

So the Beauty Card reminds you of love's disruptive power. It can strike into a tranquil and well organised life like a hawk into a dovecote. Beauty is a disruption to the organised lives people have built. Beware of the impact of the Beauty if it is related to the world of work!

The Beauty Card stands too for inspiration. Beatrice's image as a young girl inspired Dante to write the Inferno although they had hardly met. The search for perfection often in men's eyes takes the shape of a woman, driving them to conquer empires and write symphonies. The White Goddess or the Muse is another name for the same force. The Beauty Card therefore alerts us to the arts and artists .

The facets of the Beauty point us too to another area. Jung taught us that each of us has, as part of our Self, both a female side, if we are man and a male side if we are a woman. In dreams and fantasies the female side – the Anima – will guide the dominant side of a man. In a woman the guiding force is the Animus. This card reminds us of this duality in our nature. (The Stranger Card corresponds to the Animus.) So the Beauty Card is there to tell some people of their hidden sensitive side.

Is Beauty skin deep? Of course not, but surfaces matter, and the Beauty Card reminds us of the importance of appearances. The adornment of our bodies is a mark of our humanity and it goes deep into pre-history. We have instincts to make things pretty and to embellish our surroundings. Style and elegance and our need for new things are all being celebrated here. Our happiness and our self esteem are linked to the way we look and our outside can change our inside.

Of course too there is another side of the card. Beauty can inspire jealousy and lead to vanity. Beware the temptation to ask too often 'Mirror, mirror on the wall'. The muse who inspires can turn into the siren who lures voyagers to the rocks. Beauty can be a bitch as well as a Virgin.

The Beauty Card tells you must expect changes when perfection enters your life story.

ASSOCIATIONS AND OPPOSITES

Romantic Love	Jealousy
Passion, love affairs	Vanity
Charm	The whore, siren, bitch
Attraction	The rival in love
Flirting	The mirror
Fascination	Inspiration
The ideal, perfection	Illusion
The anima	The White Goddess
The Arts	Cosmetics

THOUGHT PROMPTS

❖ Does your experience tell you that romantic love has to be linked to sexual love?

❖ In your experience do some beautiful woman have problems in finding happiness because of their beauty?

❖ Do you know someone who in their search for perfection or very high standards are restless and unsatisfied?

❖ Which character in a story do you associate with Beauty?

THE WARRIOR

When evil's loose who'll be your shield?
His will to win, his sword to wield.

Heroes rescue us from difficulties and dangers. They cut through problems we thought were impenetrable. They may not be smooth talkers, but they are doers. The Warrior represents them. Like the Beauty Card the Warrior's meaning depends whether the Inquirer is a man or a woman and for her it can stand as the man in her life.

In the card he stands resting on his sword outside the encampment prepared for some medieval battle. He looks as if he is the captain of his fate. Maybe he is a loner and knows that the time for talking is over and there is soon a job for him to do.

The Warrior Card stands for courage. It is not, of course, an exclusively male virtue. We all face dilemmas where we can duck the issue and back away from the situation, try a compromise, fudge it. The Warrior tells us we need bold decisive action. We must face our fears and halt our vacillations.

The Warrior has a sword. He will use it. We see force as morally indefensible in many situations and war as unthinkable, but he knows that there is a right and a wrong and his loved ones and his people must be defended. Conflict and tension in our lives cannot be wished away.

He is a winner and he tells us to be so too. It is possible to put people into categories of winners and losers. Winners get their way, come on top and have the luck. Losers always seem to be victimised by events, and be on the receiving end of what life dished out and dogged by consistent bad luck. Sometimes they choose it, because it gives them excuses for failure. The Warrior Card encourages us to make the switch.

There have always been heroes. Perseus, Theseus, Achilles, St George, Robin Hood, Siegfried, Alexander, Nelson, George Washington. Heroines too have warrior qualities: Joan of Arc, Queen Elizabeth I, Florence Nightingale. Mythical heroes follow patterns. They have a mysterious birth, rise to meteoric powers and then after their triumph are betrayed or die. The developing psyche needs to focus on a hero and the male ego needs to identify with them. The young need to win their identities in order to make an impact on the hostile world. The Warrior Card reminds us of this necessary process. It highlights the need for the will. In order to make change happen inside yourself or outside you need to take a decision, a positive commitment with a plunge into what is always an unknown situation.

As in every Psycard there is an ambivalence. The Warrior cuts through things (surgeons, butchers, mathematicians, philosophers, composers are often men) which means he may lack finesse, tact or diplomacy. He may point us to a degree of extroversion that implies a blindness about what is going on inside himself and to an insensitivity to others feelings. He may need to be rescued by the feminine part which is suppressed in his nature. Anger and aggressiveness and a propensity to quarrelling can be part of his make-up. You must be alert to these aspects. His single-mindedness can become tunnel vision. His tight control of his emotions may tell us dangerous forces are bottled up. The adjoining cards can tell you much. Will the Beauty soften him? Will the Tower suggest he is in for a fall?

Our lives often present a period of trial or ordeal. We are being tested and our futures depend on it. At these times we need the qualities of the Warrior.

ASSOCIATIONS AND OPPOSITES

Courage
Guts
The Hero   Anger
Winners   Aggression
The Will   Losers
Determination   Ruthlessness
Extroversion   Quarrelsomeness
Maleness in teenagers   Tunnel vision
Honour   Emotionally bottled up
Purpose.
Action Man

THOUGHT PROMPTS

❖ In your experience can the qualities of the Warrior Card be seen equally in women as in men?
❖ Do you know people who see themselves as losers? Can this be changed?
❖ What sort of heroes or male models do young men aspire to today, and are those models satisfying?
❖ What character on TV or in a film do you think most represents this card?

29

THE LIAR

Signals lie. So pleasing smiles beware
Who flatters you will bring despair

Someone is deceiving you. It is probably you yourself. The Liar Card alerts you that what seems is not always so, that surfaces do not reflect the realities of your situation, that the ice is thin and that masks can crack.

The card shows a jester capering round on a stage. In one hand he (she?) presents a mask very similar to his face. In the other hand a miniature mask. He is trying to win applause from his audience in some makeshift theatre.

'Anything to please' is one of the characteristics of the Liar. He reminds us of those who adjust their message or views to the prevailing situation. You doubt their sincerity because you do not understand their motives. They are plausible ; they smile and the more they smile you become suspicious.

Masks are to disguise, frighten or impress the viewer or to protect the wearer or to turn them into something else. Masks are personalities. We all 'put on a face to meet the faces that we meet'. We all need protective make-up in social situations. Our inner selves are vulnerable and we need camouflage or armour. The danger is that we cannot distinguish from the inner and the outer. We develop complex characters for ourselves that become petrified and do not allow the inner self to breathe. When the mask cracks there can be stress or even breakdown.

The Liar Card is warning us that we are not being true to our inner natures (or someone around us likewise). Extravagant jollity can belie deep pain.

Sanctimoniousness can be a mask to ruthlessness. Caring exteriors can hide callousness. Deliberate hypocrisy is not unknown, but far more common are the misleading signals that people give when they are not in touch with themselves.

We seek truth. We need to have a clear grasp of our inner selves in order to be happy and to grow, and to find the right roles in the drama we are playing. The Liar Card is pointing us to the fact that either we or someone else is mis-cast, that preconceptions and prejudices are stopping us from seeing it clearly. For instance, parents may have mistaken views about their children. 'He's like me, he can't possibly be gay'. 'She's going to be a doctor; it is a family tradition'.

There are other ways we can be deceived: rumour and gossip. 'Everyone is saying she is carrying on with someone'. There may perhaps be nothing in it, but truth is complex and rumour is distorting reality. Flattery too is another manifestation of the Liar. The aim is to puff up the ego for the advantage of the flatterer. When someone is hungry for popularity and is milking applause from their audience, the Liar is around.

The Liar Card tells us to be suspicious about words. We all know people who say all the time 'honestly' or 'to be absolutely frank'. Their words tell us they are all too often speaking with forked tongue. The lies that 'honest' Iago told to inflame Othello's jealousy were couched in a bluff soldierly way. If we read in a newspaper about an event or person which we know we can see the distortion that creeps in, not through malice, but because words mislead us. It is one of Psycards' beliefs that pictures – images that ring true in our hearts – tell us more truth.

Words, masks, the personas we develop are often necessary protective screens. The Liar Card asks you to look underneath them.

ASSOCIATIONS AND OPPOSITES

The Mask	The True Self
Misleading Signals	Pictures & Images
Hidden motives	
Insincerity Rumour and Gossip	Prejudice
Flattery	
Easy popularity	The personality
Newspaper reports	Smokescreens
Being given flannel	

THOUGHT PROMPTS

❖ Do you know people who often unconsciously give misleading signals about their character?
❖ What masks are your friends or family wearing?
❖ Are they deliberately deceptive or necessary protection?
❖ Can you think of examples of people whose speech and language has deliberate smokescreens?
❖ Which person on TV do you think reflects this card?

30

THE STRANGER

*Bid welcome in. Never ignore
Who knocks upon your heart's door*

Will there be a knock on the door? Will there be someone there you don't know? Will someone visit you in the night? Don't worry. It's a friend. The Stranger Card tells us that our organised patterns can be disrupted by disturbing and exciting outside influences.

There he stands in the picture as the door opens. Or is it a she?. At the door is this character who seeks to talk to you. He (or she) is dressed in this mysterious way. Is he in distress? He has come out of the night and he bids to enter our lives.

The Stranger Card has several linked messages for us. Dreams are one. Some people can remember nothing but a meaningless jumble of images when they wake. Others say they don't dream at all. We may be too busy to untangle them. In myths and Bible stories and in hundreds of documented historical cases dreams have shaped people's lives. Joseph's dreams got him out of prison and into Pharaoh's palace. Joan of Arc's placed her at the head of an army and eventually at the stake. We are told that dreams come from the unconscious. It is only in the last hundred years that we started talking about the unconscious and maybe it is a way of avoiding another truth, known to our ancestors for some ten thousand years. God or angels or guardian spirits or demons or outside intelligences speak to us in dreams. Not only to Joseph and Joan of Arc but to each of us. We know perfectly well when we answer the phone there is a person talking to us, and we would laugh knowingly at any savage who told us the telephone instrument itself was communicating to us. How come we treat the unconscious as magic? The Stranger Card tells us to listen, listen, listen to the garbled messages that get through to us. Physiologists recognise that our brains have an ancient side and a new one. Human beings are radios attuned to more than one station.

In every community we build up rules, habits, attitudes and prejudices that bind us together and on a social level we are instinctively prone to exclude strangers who seek to enter into our circle. The higher religions enjoin us to welcome them (the story of Ruth in the Bible is an example). There are also social and biological reasons. Enclosed communities die. Outside pollination is vital for growth. Families that are too close breed trouble. Incest taboos in tribal societies bear witness to that. So at a day-to-day level the Stranger Card can tell us to welcome people of different background, race and origin from ourselves and to be open to our in-laws and to see another dimension in those nearest to us.

It is equally true in terms of our psyches. Jung's philosophy teaches us to find our true self, and that life is a journey towards individuation, where all parts of our nature coalesce and we find wholeness. On the road, the 'ego' needs help. Inside him or herself is a shadow self of the other sex: for men the 'Anima', for women the 'Animus'. These guides emerge in dreams and fantasies and prompt intuitions and new directions. The Stranger Card stands for the 'Animus' or 'Anima'.

There is a fundamental rule. Circles need to be

broken up by straight lines. Yin (the female principle) and yang (the male principle) interpenetrate, as do sperm and ovum; as do bees and flowers; as barbarians intrude into dying civilisations.

When your door bell rings who will it be? A Jehovah's Witness? An extra-terrestrial? Or your long-lost brother?

ASSOCIATIONS AND OPPOSITES

Opening doors	Prejudice
Dreams	Exclusion
The anima, the animus	Slamming doors
Change	The family circle
Welcoming Opportunity	
Angels	Devils
Hearing Inner Voices	Schizophrenia
Psychic Gifts	

THOUGHT PROMPTS

❖ Do you know anyone who has psychic gifts?
❖ Do you listen to your dreams?
❖ Can you think of examples where closing a door in your life stopped the possibility of growth?
❖ What would a stranger look like if your doorbell rang?

31

THE SAGE

Forget the fancies of the hour
Ancient wisdom has more power

This card offers you the antidote to a powerful drug that may be poisoning your mind. The Sage takes the heat of feverish passion that on occasion sweeps dangerously through our lives. It represents age-old wisdom and prudence.

The Card depicts an old, white-bearded man in his study, surrounded by leather-bound books of knowledge handed down generation by generation. On the desk stand the phials, retorts and scales. Perhaps he is an alchemist who strives to purify base metal into gold, or maybe he is a wise hermit in his cell, or a philosopher who knows the wisdom of the East.

There are times when we need outside help, in order to extricate ourselves from deep holes, often of our own digging. The Sage provides the advice and authority we need. This may come in the shape of an experienced friend, a counsellor, a doctor or a lawyer, someone wise in the way of the world, who can see our problems in a detached way.

Many of our problems arise from passion. Think of passion as powerful psychical gusts like a little tornado that wreaks havoc in our own lives and in the lives of others. It can be sexual desires fixated onto another, which have no hope for happiness or fulfilment. It can be obsessional hatred or burning resentment or money urges or gambling fevers or a compulsion of one kind or another. Those who are victims of passion need outside dispassionate help.

The Sage Card tells us to detach ourselves from our problems or to seek someone else to do it for us. The

Sage has seen it all before. He or she will be able to draw on a body of experience to understand the specific situation we are in. That is what a doctor or a lawyer does. The Sage can tap into a fund of established knowledge. You can be sure that any advice you are given has no strings attached. You are not being sold anything. Wisdom usually comes free.

We are today at the mercy of fads and fancies, of new trends or media reports that sway our opinions or our bodies, our food habits, our sex lives or our morality. The Sage is tuned into different frequencies. Under the ripples of the surface lie the depths of truth.

There are different levels of knowledge. If you want help with your computer you need know-how. There is also a clever and sophisticated knowledge of how the world works and again this is a marvellous gift. But wisdom sees into your heart with objectivity and kindness and can see the short-term in a bright eternal light.

The Sage Card may stand for the grand-parents. Parents and children always generate tension between themselves. Grand-parents can present a valuable detachment from a problem and give a multigenerational perspective.

You see the Sage as someone teaching and preaching, offering solutions to an awed audience. Maybe this is true. But the Sage Card also has a quieter aspect. Before you teach you have to learn. Before you give you listen. Before you do anything you need preparation. The Sage is not being wise; he is becoming wise. This is a card about development; about recognising your own deficiencies and weaknesses. It is about humility. A Zen master said 'When the student is ready the teacher will appear.'

The Sage tells you to pay no heed to those who have an axe to grind. Listen to the quiet voice of wisdom.

ASSOCIATIONS AND OPPOSITES

Wisdom	Being trendy
Knowledge	Slick smartness
Professionalism	The passions
Old Age	Youth
Detachment	Knowing it all
Grandparents	
Humility	
Merlin	
Listening,	Talking
Teaching	Preaching
Prudence	
Caution	

THOUGHT PROMPTS

❖ Do you believe your own parents can teach something to your children?

❖ Can you think of situations in your own life where a professional might provide a new perspective to your problem?

❖ Who do you know who most reflects the qualities of the Sage Card?

❖ In your experience what sort of wise counsel is of most use in stressful situations?

32

THE FOOL

*Some cheer some fear some sneer some jeer
But it's truth he tells if you can hear*

There is no shortage of fools in our lives – fumblers, bumblers or people puffed up with their own self importance. Why does Psycards need a Fool among its characters? Because he won't take seriously most of the things that worry us, and because he's happy. He gives us a clue to find happiness ourselves.

The picture shows he is dancing, fluting his songs along what looks like a cliff edge. Certainly no natty dresser, his clothes are tattered and torn. The house perched perilously on the cliff may be his house – or is it our own (mortgage and all) or even our civilisation? He is dancing to a different tune from the rest of us and he does not mind if the powers to be tut tut about him or the children gawk at him. He is a travelling musician perhaps, or a hippie or a neglected poet or a Pied Piper.

One of the messages of the Fool Card is that you cannot plan your happiness. Sometimes it happens. Sensible people have jobs and mortgages and marriages and homes and responsibilities but these do not necessarily make them happy. You cannot track happiness like a hunter after your prey. Happiness refuses to go in straight predictable lines. (It dances around like a butterfly and alights where it chooses on some lucky flower.)

So there are times in your life when you need to go off at a tangent and do something that everyone tells you is irresponsible. Leave your job, become an artist, buy a caravan, take a surprise holiday, fall in love with someone unsuitable. There are times when you need to trust yourself and not be governed by conventions.

The Fool Card is about playing, regressing to one's child-like self, doing things for their own sake not for calculated gain. It points us to fantasy and day-dreaming and out of that may grow creativity. Many great enterprises and inventions are born this way – like Newton's apple, or Robert the Bruce's spider. No momentous project can be undertaken without some 'fool' who said to him or herself. 'Just imagine that...' or 'If only things were different....' Wish and it can come true. This card is encouraging you to close your eyes and relax and think the most marvellous and impossible things for yourself. .

The card has other strong aspects of meaning. It alerts us to the importance of the arts. The Fool is telling us that there are other values to cherish in a materialist world. He stands for inspiration.

Trend-setters often start off as fools. Maybe one of the negative aspects about the Fool Card is that it warns us of those apparently charismatic characters who lead their followers to a dance which leaves the leader a whole lot richer.

Think of him too as a comedian. More truth can be told about the world in jokes. Kings in medieval times kept a court fool who was allowed to say the unsayable where other courtiers might fear the executioner. The Fool Card asks you to listen to the jokes that people tell because there may be truth in them.

There is yet another message. The Fool trusts the universe and the people around him. He is confident that the world will look after him and he has no worries about where his next meal will come from. St Francis was called a Holy Fool and he heightened the spirituality of the Middle Ages. The Fool can stand for the Christian gift of Faith.

If there is a Fool around you laugh at him or her. You may not take everything they say as serious, but ask yourself whether they are suggesting an alternative sort of happiness.

ASSOCIATIONS AND OPPOSITES

Innocence	Materialism
Happiness	The rat race
Creativity	Tunnel Vision
Inspiration	Playing safe
Humour	
Music	
Childlike enthusiasm	
Daydreaming	
Visionaries	False prophets
Playing Hippies	Squares
Trust	Suspicion

THOUGHT PROMPTS

❖ When did you last daydream and fantasise about your future?
❖ Do you know people who have deliberately rejected the rat race and found their own sort of happiness?
❖ Do you think it is easy to distinguish between straight stupidity and the behaviour of the Fool?
❖ Do you like the Fools you have encountered in your life – or do they rather irritate you?

33

THE BEAST

Call your courage up to slay
The foul fiend who bars the way

S t. George had his dragon. Jack had his giant. Theseus had the Minotaur. You may need your beast. Know it well. Study the malevolent creature like a hunter. This is one of the messages of the Beast Card.

The card depicts a fierce scaly mythological monster spitting hatred, fuming with anger and ready to lash out. The picture is fiery with sulphurous reds.

The Beast is your personal beast. It is what you have to contend with in your life. You have killed it several times but often it is completely unkillable. Probably it comes from your childhood, even from the womb. It is the beast that creaked outside your bedroom, that lurked around when your parents were out of the house, that bullied you at school, that threatened to maim and stunt your growth, that changed into the illnesses that beset you. It is behind the traumas that psychoanalysts search for, the suppressed memories and the child abuse. Beast are ugly things and leave blighted lives and emotional carnage. For some people the Beast erupts as anger with oneself and anger projected out onto others. For others it is a feeling of rejection or inadequacy and failure that accompanies them all their lives. It manifests itself in asthma, eczema, back pain, eating disorder. The scar tissue can be seen in the body language.

The Beast Card is then telling us to know our enemies. The Beast is most dangerous when it lurks in its lair, when its smell of fear pervades the air. Once it can be coaxed out into bright sunlight and we can see its lurid colours and look into its evil eyes we can then have a chance to overcome it. So make it come out and fight. Objectify it, visualise it , make it concrete.

Do we need the Beast? Maybe we do. One reason is that we cannot have heroes without challenges. As discussed with the Warrior Card, the ego needs to prove him or herself. It can only develop its true self by overcoming danger. The Beast is in a way part of ourselves and we can only be our true selves in our struggle with the rejected part. Symbiosis – a working relationship held by built-in tension – exists between Self and Beast. On every medal and picture book St George is locked together with his dragon. Maybe they are friends..

The Beast turns into another useful animal: a scapegoat, that wretched creature that is cast out from the safety and security of our herd or community that carries upon itself all our misdemeanours, leaving us somehow cleansed. It is a sacrifice. We expel our fears and unacceptable desires onto another group or person who can be justifiably hated. (Children project their fears of an encroaching and threatening world and transform them into friendly-frightening dinosaurs that can be eaten in potato snacks) The Beast reminds us of this process. It tells us to neutralise it by being aware of how it works.

The Beast represents a lot of the blatant sins we can find in others or ourselves. It is anger , spite-spitting hatred, cruelty, lust, greed and sloth. Despair must also be included. Think of it also as your bad habits that will not be easily beaten. Heroin perhaps, more likely tobacco, alcohol and cream cakes. The Beast's scaly hide makes it resistant save only to steely determination.

Welcome the Beast Card. Remember it is only when we see the 'other' – the Minotaurs, the ogre, the Gorgon – that we know we are truly human..

ASSOCIATIONS AND OPPOSITES

Fears Phobias	
Despair	Hope
Bad Habits	Heroes
Violence	Saints
The Scapegoat	Moral Weapons
Courage	
The Irrational	
The Seven Deadly Sins	
Childhood Terrors	
	Growing up
	The Big Challenge
Monsters	Our Humanity

THOUGHT PROMPTS

❖ What most frightened you as a child?
❖ Can you identify your own personal Beast?
❖ What sort of ways can you fight the Beast? What weaponry do you think is most effective?
❖ What person in your life do you most represent with the Beast?

34

THE MESSAGE

*Someone is calling from somewhere
If you can see, if you can hear*

omeone somewhere is trying to get through to you? Are you on the line? Is your receiver off the hook? The Message Card is trying to tell you.

This is the first of the seven Psycard 'Happenings'. They stand for major psychic events in your life when 'Characters' 'Symbols' 'Archetypes' and' Fundamentals' all impinge. The card depicts the catch hauled on the deck by the fishermen and includes a bottle with its message. Is some castaway on a desert island pleading to be rescued? Will it contain the treasure map? Or will the fisherman chuck it back into the sea?

The ocean is the unconscious, its fishes darting with symbolic life, and its tides are always throwing us apparently random messages. So the Message Card is alerting us to be prepared for incoming signals from our inner depths. They can manifest themselves in dreams, in fantasies, in art and music, in curious coincidences, in our own body language (Could that muscular twinge tell us of a spiritual hunger?) Even the behaviour of our cats and dogs and the birds in our garden can be fraught with meaning.

In a week we are lucky to receive one 'real' letter in the post amid the junk mail and the bills. Every day we are bombarded with hundreds of messages from advertisers, and we know how to filter them out of our consciousness. We are washed in a torrent of sensory inputs which we have to interpret. Yet maybe in our entire lives we will receive some ten messages or so that will transform our futures, pointing us to opportunities, leading us to loved ones, offering us hope, or warning us of impending danger. How can we be sure that the right messages get through to us? Psychologists tell us (in the theory of Cognitive Dissonance) that we build defences against anything that disturbs the model we have made of the world, and that we censor and tune out unwelcome news or anything that threatens our status quo.

Jesus told his messages in parables. The truths in symbols, ritual, dreams, art creations, plays and stories have more chance of getting through our defences if they come in disguise or dressed up . Some of the most important messages we receive have to be in a sort of code. The Message Card encourages us, therefore, to start decoding the world around us and in ourselves.

In the same way if we want to transmit a message to someone ('I love you...' ... 'things are bad'... 'I need space...') we may need to communicate them in a different way and to change the medium. A bunch of flowers may be more effective than mere words in some contexts.

All communication is fragile between human beings and if we are able to open up ourselves to others a high degree of sensitivity and subtlety is needed. We need to listen for incoming messages and leave space for them. Meditation and prayer, relaxation and holidays are some of the times we can sometimes pick up more clearly the psychic traffic from within ourselves.

An Iroquois hunter can see a bent blade of grass and know where to find his quarry. A detective can pick up a thread of hair and solve a crime. They are receiving messages. In a rich and complex universe maybe we are being 'talked to' in many other ways. Our forefathers not so long ago believed that angels and spirits were talking to us. Maybe there is a psychic 'Internet' which we can tap into. But the Message Card tells us that a message in a bottle will be landing on your deck.

ASSOCIATIONS AND OPPOSITES

Communication	Dis-information
Coding /decoding	The media
Bridges between conscious and unconscious	
Signals	Isolation
Information	
Clues	
Angels	
The right channels	TV Channels
Tuning in	
Sensitivity	
Listening	Censorship.

THOUGHT PROMPTS

❖ If an angel wanted to talk to you how could they do it?
❖ Do you know people whose body language is giving different messages from their words?
❖ What letter or phone call have you ever had that completely altered the direction of your life?
❖ What message now would you most like to receive?

35

THE VOYAGE

Your heart turns to a new shore
With new horizons to explore

The wind is blowing. Pack up your suitcase. Dust off your passport from the bottom drawer. You are going on a journey. But remember that journeys don't necessarily start with travel brochures and airport lounges. There are journeys of the heart too.

The Journey Card shows a galleon in full sail upon a sparkling sea setting course for a mysterious shore that the mariners' charts have plotted. Maybe it is seeking spices or gold or imperial power or a new home or maybe prompted by mere curiosity.

A hundred years ago only the rich and sailors or soldiers travelled to foreign countries and it was an adventure to visit a relative fifty miles away. Now we pack-back through continents and book second holidays. But the Air Miles we clock up do not relate to the psychological distances we travel. The Voyage Card reminds us of this. A voyage changes you. On arrival you are not the person who set out. You change your opinions of yourself and your travelling companions.

Maybe one simple message of the Voyage Card for anyone setting on their holiday is to treat it like an adventure, a quest even a pilgrimage. You are not just shipping your body to the sun, but instead embarking on a journey of the heart and mind where you'll find new friends and challenges.

Holidays are one thing. This card could be telling you that you are now ready to make a voyage of the mind or spirit. There are times in our lives when we need roots. (The Tree Card tells us that.) There are others when we need horizons. This may be prompted by restlessness or dissatisfaction with your present life. You may know there is something better somewhere else. You may see opportunities for fame and fortune. This may manifest in going to Australia or to moving five hundred yards up the road or changing your life style. Drifting is the negative. The Voyage is the positive.

A voyager needs to shed surplus baggage. If we travel psychologically light, we will be free of sentiments, illusions, hang-ups and trivial worries. We will be physically fit. And it means saying goodbye for a while to friends and families. 'He travels the furthest who travels alone'.

In the Middle Ages the travelling instinct was channelled into pilgrimage. (The shell that was the sign of the pilgrim turned itself into the Shell Petrol station). Islam enjoins believers to make a visit to Mecca and the holy places once in their lifetime. The pilgrim gained spiritual merit in visiting a shrine where a saint was buried like Canterbury or Lourdes.

Because all life is a voyage. You change. The scenery changes. Travelling companions appear and disappear. Maybe at the end there is 'the haven where we would be'. If we think of own death as a voyage where we embark on a new and maybe hazardous adventure it may alter our perception of our old age. We should be packing up. Van Gogh called the illnesses that kill us as 'our tickets to the stars'. Instead of clinging to the world around us we should prepare for a new one.' Old men should be explorers', TS Eliot has told us. The Buddhist

Sanyasa doctrine tells believers at the latter part of their lives, once their responsibilities to their families are fulfilled, to travel as beggars.

So the Voyage Card says 'Bon Voyage' to you. You may encounter perils, have love affairs, shed illusions, meet strange people – and eventually find you heart aching for home.

ASSOCIATIONS AND OPPOSITES

Travelling	Drifting
New Horizons	Escapism
Pilgrimage	
Quest	
Adventure	Dead ends
Curiosity	Stability
Exploring	Roots
Romantic Urges	Restlessness
	Ship wreck

Shedding encumbrances
Planning new directions

THOUGHT PROMPTS

❖ Are you a 'roots' person or a 'journey' person?
❖ Should a holiday for you be pure relaxation or is it more enjoyable if you have other goals?
❖ Which person among your friends and families needs to be influenced by the Voyage Card?
❖ Do you know people whose Voyage has met with disaster and others who have found a new country?

36

THE PUZZLE

*Who Why Where How Which Whither When
Blind choice must be the lot of men*

'I don't know which way to go' 'Look at the map' 'The map tells me nothing' 'Follow your instinct' 'My instinct tells me nothing'

That is the puzzle: those situations in life where your heart is undecided, you've weighed up all the pros and cons, and no balance appears, and no oracle will give you clear answers – yet you still have to act. Do you go back? Do you go forward?

The card shows two identical doors in a mysterious courtyard set in a forest. Between the doors a statue queen dangles one key. The forest represents your encircling doubt. The queen is the imperious need to make a decision. The silence waits... What do you do? Walk away?

Does the left door open onto horrors unnamed? Does the right contain the treasure you are seeking? Do they both lead to the same chamber? Is the whole situation a set-up?

The Puzzle Card is telling us of a blockage to our plans and progress. This can often indicate a communication barrier between conscious and unconscious. The ego wants one thing. The unconscious wants something else. The result is paralysis of decision-making powers and frustration. Maybe the answer is to wait and hope that inspiration comes. Time certainly decides a lot of things. But we all know that we cannot dodge a pressing issue or leave it forever in the psyche's in-tray.

Another answer (and with the Puzzle Card we cannot expect direct solutions) is the application of lateral thinking. We see problems as being set in concrete with fixed elements embedded into them. If we think of the problem not as a football stadium but more as a river with changing banks with new forces flowing in, we can perhaps see a new perspective.

This card perhaps encourages us when we are on the horns of a dilemma to make an act of will. The will is when the self leaps into the deep end. You have weighed up all the balance of possibilities. You have noted that all the signals are confusing and you are being given conflicting advice. It is up to you alone – and you act. That is the existentialist philosophy that outlines that you decide your own fate by such acts and thereby win true freedom.

A story is told of Alexander the Great who was challenged to untie the Gordian Knot, an intricately tangled rope that could only be untied by the ruler of the world. Alexander slashed it with his sword. When we are faced with puzzles in our lives either direct action or lateral thinking can provide answers. Sometimes hard nuts mean nut crackers.

Puzzles, dilemmas, barriers are sometimes asking us to play games with them. The Sphinx was an unpleasant monster who devoured Thebans who could not answer her riddles. 'What goes on four feet ,two feet , and three feet and the more feet it goes on the weaker it is?' Oedipus told her it was Man, with the old man with his stick making the three legs.

A puzzle is a challenge. The Puzzle Card asks you to solve it when you are faced with two doors in the forest.

ASSOCIATIONS AND OPPOSITES

Uncertainty	Panic
Dilemma	Vacillation
Necessity to make a decision	Dilly Dallying
Blockage	
Question	
Doubt	Frustration
The test or examination	
Riddles	
Hard Nuts	

THOUGHT PROMPTS

❖ Have you come across a specific major Puzzle in your life?

❖ Have you had periods in your life when you could not make decisions? What caused it? How did it resolve itself?

❖ Do you know people who faced with a dilemma made a choice and got it wrong?

❖ Is there a time when if you do nothing the 'puzzle' disappears of its own accord?

37

PRISON

*The door clangs shut. Who holds the key
To win you back your liberty?*

You are trapped in some cruel situation. How long is your sentence? What were you guilty of ? What hope or reassurance can you find? Are you absolutely sure you are not your own gaoler? The Prison Card asks you some of these questions.

The card shows a prisoner shackled miserably in some dungeon viewed through the bars. Through the little window high up in the wall the sun streams in. The Card is a mirror of the Liberation Card and the two can be considered as a 'before' and 'after'

Psycards works by images, metaphors and similes. It is unlikely that you are in prison, but you may feel that it applies to one aspect of your life or someone else's. Prison can mean being trapped into a relationship or a marriage that seems like a life sentence. You may be shackled by a disability or ill health. Your job may be a dead end or a constriction of your real talents. Your home situation may stop you developing. You cannot do what you want to do because of family constraints. And of course poverty is a prison too.

Some of the questions the Card asks is what crime are you in for, were you guilty of it, and who is your gaoler. Indeed the Card raises the whole question of punishment. Society punishes criminals for retribution, as a deterrent, and to protect itself from dangerous people. Very often as individuals we get punished by the consequences of our actions. (If we cause car accidents our premium insurance increases. If we drink too much we feel sick.) Very often we punish ourselves through a feeling of guilt and shame. A perception of failure and inadequacy can shackle us like a ball and chain. We can put ourselves into stretches of solitary confinement refusing to unbutton our problems to our friends and families. We are burdened by a feeling of what our grandparents would call a sense of sin.

The Prison Card then in these situations pleads for 'Leniency, My Lord'. Self-acceptance is the key to unlocking the prison door.

Maybe this is too easy for many for whom the door clangs shut on their cell. The Prison Card seeks to remind us how we can endure the sentence before us. What are your options? Hitler and John Bunyan wrote world-changing books in prison. Solzhenitsyn wrote his exposé of Stalinist camps from inside a gulag, smuggled out on tiny scraps of paper. In the Bible Joseph had a dream which results in his release and his elevation to Pharaoh's palace. Prisons force one to go inside oneself and can release the powers of the unconscious. It provides enforced time for self-education and to learn the skills that can be put to use when freedom is eventually achieved. Whether you make friends with the sparrows at your bars or practise transcendental meditation the physical constraints of prison can encourage your growth in other ways.

Remember too that people in chains can be dangerous. They nurture revenge. Like Samson they can suddenly break out and wreak destruction. Dumas' hero in *The Count of Monte Cristo* is given the secret by a cell-mate to acquire immense wealth. On his escape he executes his revenge.

The Prison Card therefore reminds us that being confined means the deprivation of light. It is in darkness that seeds germinate. Day follows night. You may not be in control, but there are other forces at work that can bring you release from your cell.

ASSOCIATIONS AND OPPOSITES

Being trapped	
Loneliness	
Darkness	Light
At the mercy of events	Liberation
Dead Time	
Punishment	
Guilt and Shame	
Failure	
Inadequacy	A Victim of Authority

THOUGHT PROMPTS

❖ If you were in prison what would you do? Plan your escape? Write a book? Plot your revenge? Or what?

❖ Do you know people who are trapped by a situation they cannot control, yet who could in fact release themselves if they know how?

❖ In your experience how do people overcome their feelings of guilt?

❖ Which person whom you know would you match up with the Prison Card?

38

LIBERATION

Up and away at long last free
But where tonight will your bed be?

Liberation is joy and the exhilaration of breaking free from situations that bind us – but it warns of dangers.

The card depicts the open door of the bleak fortress; and galloping away across the moat in the cold dawn are – two figures. Has the prisoner escaped or has he or she been rescued? Have two lovers sped away from some domineering patriarch? The door was open and the key in the lock, so maybe an insider has engineered their escape. Where they are going we know not. Let us hope for their sake they know.

The Liberation Card is enabling. It tell us to do our own thing and grow in our own way and break free of the constriction that stunts our growth.

There are precious times in our lives when we enjoy this feeling: most obviously when we are breaking through out of childhood into adulthood. Maybe it is when we dangle our first car key in our fingers. Maybe it is entering retirement, and even (it is possible) at the prospect of death. On a Friday night in a small way many of us have a feeling of liberation.

Freedom raises the question of freedom *from* what and freedom *for* what and it needs to be distinguished from running away which can be evading challenges. Liberation can be letting the arrow loose from the bow so it speeds to its target. Or it can be opening the window for a butterfly to escape. Both are good, right and necessary. But where you are let free you need to ask where are you going to. Freedom may mean a Gretna Green elopement that can blight two lives. Any prisoner on discharge or escapee on the run needs a safe home. Freedom, like prison, can be lonely: if you escape you are at the mercy of predatory forces all around you. On a basic level a 15 year old who liberates him or herself from home is in dire danger.

The Liberation Card then suggests you treat the period of liberation as a narrow time-window. In the first euphoric stage you feel you will be in control for ever; but it won't last. You will need to make decisions and commitments sooner than you wish. If you are going to survive freedom you are going to need discipline. In an individual's life there are perhaps less than ten key decisions when you have moral freedom and where you can shape what sort of person you are. Every other moment leads up to those critical turning points.

There are other ways of looking at the Liberation Card. It can be seen as the Self striving to develop. In order to find its true identity it needs to see the unconscious as dark forces of a prison. We know that the true Self needs to find integration and harmony between conscious and unconscious. So maybe there is significance that the fortress door in the card is open; maybe the prisoner's escape was encouraged.

There is still a further aspect of the card. Freedom is the Spirit. Prison is Matter. Ariel in the Tempest seeks to break free of Prospero's controls; free spirits chafe against the impositions of the world. Yet Spirit needs to be put to work in Matter, in the physical body. Only in death can it be free.

So this card bids you be free. Maybe it asks whether you are a budgerigar who will be pounced on by the cat when he hops out of the cage. Or a hawk spiralling free yet responsive to the calls of the falconer.

ASSOCIATIONS AND OPPOSITES

Freedom from...
Freedom to...
Running Away
Adolescence Joy   Gloom
Release
A window of opportunity
The need for choice
The Spirit   Matter
The light
Breaking away   Conventions
The first awareness of the true Self

THOUGHT PROMPTS
❖ Do you remember your first feeling of liberation?
❖ How many times in your life have you been truly free?
❖ Do you know people who have had the feeling of freedom but their situation has led them to a worse prison?
❖ Which character do you think in the 20th Century most represents Liberation?

39

THE CAVE

Ponder deep inside your soul
Darkness can sometimes make you whole

The Cave tells us there is a time for withdrawal, for secrecy and the healing power of darkness. We go into caves for protection. We go out to change the world.

The cards depicts a figure crouched in the inner recesses of a cave, sheltered in the gloom far from the entrance where the sun does not penetrate. Is the figure in despair or in prayer ? The position is foetus-like and we cannot see if any clothes are worn.

The Cave is the womb from where we all came. It is natural enough that the earliest man sought caves as their dwelling, not just because it gave them a roof over their heads. It provided safety from predatory animals and enemies. They had a vantage point, because caves are set in hills, and they could scan the plain for their quarry, and from the heights sally down to hunt, then scurry back to safety. The Cave Card reminds us that there are times in our lives when we need security and to go back inside ourselves before we can venture out again.

The revolutionary who will overturn the current regime will hide in the caves till the time comes when he descends to head the popular insurrection. David in the Bible gathered his forces against Saul from the cave, and it was there that Robert the Bruce watched the persistent spider spin its web and was reminded to try again in his campaign against his enemies.

There are some people who have a temperament that is as equable and unvaried as a broad plain. Others have ups and downs, mountains and valleys, and suffer mood swings. If you are in the latter category the Cave card may alert you to a 'down' time, a feeling of depression, what Churchill called the 'Black Dog'.

Illness too can for some people be a cave – a strategy they can adopt to accomplish what they seek. This is a different from 'shamming'. An illness or a disease can allow a person to develop other areas of the personality. The achievements of Florence Nightingale to make changes in Victorian health policy were linked to the way she functioned from her sickbed. Marcel Proust's asthma caused him to withdraw to a cork-lined room insulated from the outside world where he wrote his masterpiece. Headaches can be a good reason to do the things you choose not to do. The bedroom can be a cave out of which you can emerge to astound the world.

The Cave Card reminds us of the importance of reflection. Introverts have their mental processes centred on their inner selves and on abstractions, while extroverts are geared to the outside world and other people. It is possible to move from one to the other and the Cave can signify you are moving more into an introvert mode.

There are other aspects of the Cave. It is about darkness. While growth needs sun, germination needs darkness. The unconscious past can feed the self today. There is a time for secrecy. If ideas or hopes or plans get to the outside world too early they can be scorched and die. The Cave Card tells us to nurse the precious things and keep them locked away till the time is ripe. Cave art, that mysterious depiction of animals painted by oil lamps in cave interiors, were probably a process of 'visualisation'. The concentration on the pictures of the herd of deer made it happen for real. The secret recesses of the cave inspired the action under the sun in the plains below.

So if you find yourself in the Cave don't curl up and die. Caves are numinous places where hermits live and prophetesses utter oracles and ancient treasures can be found.

ASSOCIATIONS AND OPPOSITES

Withdrawal	The Social world
Introversion	
Depression	
Illness	
Protection	
Moodiness	Equanimity
The Womb	
Darkness	
Oracles	
The current regime	
Treasure	
Secrecy	Openness
Shyness	

THOUGHT PROMPTS

❖ Do you know people who have cyclical feelings of depression?

❖ Can you find in your own life periods where you sought withdrawal from stressful situations?

❖ Do you find that going back into the past can help you handle the present?

❖ Are there periods when you need to cut yourself off from the social world?

40

UNION

Where two in one together flow
Joy's consummation you will know

The last of the Psycard pack is Union. It promises togetherness and wholeness – the bringing together of men and women, yin and yang, conscious and unconscious, the warring elements of the self, and it suggests your inner energies are combining to a nobler and fuller life.

The card depicts the spot where two bubbling mountain streams combine and at that point a silver chalice lies in the grass. The two streams are two energy flows. The waters will merge to a river that feeds through to the ocean. The chalice or loving cup puts a heavenly blessing on the natural union.

Marriage is what happens in the last act of Shakespeare comedies or Jane Austen novels or fairy stories or Mills and Boon romances (at least the older ones). It is different from relationships which mean an alliance and an agreement between two parties, but it means that each party maintains their identity, Whereas a marriage means a new entity has been formed.

What happens between man and woman is symbolic of what happens in other areas: in religion, politics, and all human affairs. A coming together is blessed, sanctioned and approved by Heavens and Earth, Church and State, in a way that fits into a whole. The Union Card points to a faith that things make sense, that there is a pattern, that heaven is passionately concerned with earth, that what is above is mirrored by what is below, and that 'all manner of things shall be well'. Natural enough that unions of all sorts be celebrated in banquets and feasts with dancing and the accompaniment of merriment and joy.

The message of the Union Card is relevant in other areas. It is pointing us to creativity. A new idea or invention or a work of art is conceived by the reconciliation of opposites, by marrying one set of assumptions or associations with another. When the two streams merge there is the new. 'Thesis' is met with 'antithesis' and they combine into 'synthesis'. That is the rhythm that Hegel and Marx applies to history and ideas. Yin and Yang the female and the male principles interact in Chinese philosophy too creating the wholeness of mind, body and spirit.

On a day to day basis the Union Card reminds us to marry up separate elements and to find new connections. This means breaking moulds and looking around for a wider perspective. Reconciliation is another message of the card. It reminds us to make peace. That means more than patching up a quarrel or fudging a compromise. There is maybe a third way out of the conflict of two warring parties. Harmony can come from two dis-chords. One and one can add up to three.

The Union Card points us too to self- development that comes to marrying the diverse elements within ourselves. We all seek to turn into what we can really be. The Self goes on a journey, confronts dangers and seeks to find its true identity. This wholeness comes from the reconciliation of conscious and unconscious. The bubbling spring and its energy forces merge into the river which unites itself to the sea.

Life and death combine in wholeness. The 'I'nquirer is the first card of the psycard pack is seeking 'I'dentity and has found it in wholeness and Union in the last card.

ASSOCIATIONS AND OPPOSITES

Wholeness Togetherness	Alienation
Integration	Atomisation
Marriage	Divorce
Synthesis	Separation
Harmony	Break-up
The Dance	
Celebration	
The Development of the Self	
Creativity	
The Complete Picture	
The Gestalt	
The Solution	

THOUGHT PROMPTS

❖ In your experience does marriage matter?
❖ Can you think of examples where bringing separate sorts of people together produces beneficial results?
❖ Are there occasions where preserving identities are more important than merging them?
❖ What are the down side risks when Unions do not 'gel'?
❖ Can you think of characters or couples who represent or embody the Union Card?

Using Psycards

*In this section the assumption is made that you are the
Inquirer and that you are reading Psycards for yourself. If
you are counselling somebody or 'reading the cards' for
someone, your client is the Inquirer.*

You are alone. No loud music is playing. No one
is clamouring for your attention. You are relaxed
and your alpha waves are washing over you. You
unwrap in expectation the forty pristine cards in the
Psycards pack. You fan them out. You pick out one or
two images. Pretty, you say. And what then?

This section tries to answer some of your questions.
The trouble is that there isn't a way to play Psycards like
Monopoly. There are absolutely no rules laid down on
high by the Psycards Central Committee. There are no

certainties, no rights and wrongs. (If the Death Card comes up next to the Mother Card it should set no alarm bells in the family!) Psycards can and hope to say some very clear and obvious truths, because directness and simplicity is built into them. Some people will pick up the cards and find they are sparking off messages for them immediately, though others will not. There are no score cards, no winners and losers, and no objective answers, because the essence of Psycards is that you create the rules to suit yourself, and that you are the most honest critic of yourself, and the sole referee of how the game is going in the arena of your heart. Suggested below are a series of exercises to use with Psycards and how to mould them and adapt them to your own life.

Exercise 1: The In-forming.

In the description of the individual cards you may note the words 'maybe' and 'perhaps' recur; cards give you 'pointers'; they alert you to possibilities; they have 'aspects'. Psycards are ambivalent. There are no apologies here. Symbols are vessels and you have to pour into them your own meaning. They are often a cloudy mirror to your own inner landscape. You have to put a value on each card in your own emotional currency.

So first, in a disciplined way, go through each card and see what it is saying to you in relation to your own life, your family, your own experience, your own impressions. The Mother Card asks you to think of your actual mother, of the very chair in which she sat in that house where you used to live years ago. The Body Card asks you to picture your own body with its bumps, its blemishes and its beauty. The Beast Card asks you to think of the times you were really frightened when you were young. The Message Card asks you to think of how wonderful it would be if at this very moment the phone rang and....

And so on. Some will perhaps not say very much to you. If so, don't worry. Put them aside for another time but relate every person close to you to one card, maybe arbitrarily. The meaning of the cards may change for you over time, and it is suggested that you note your thoughts and associations and monitor how they change.

Exercise 2: The Linking

Now you have put a personal value on individual cards, you can combine or link cards, and it is suggested you follow one rule. If any two or more cards are together they have to be either alongside or above or below each other. Following common-sense patterns (and in accordance with Tarot) it seems sensible to see the past flowing into the present, into the future as left to right; and what is underlying or unconscious or hidden is below; and what is aspired to, or belongs to our higher nature is above. Psycards suggests that you stick with this grammar. Some Tarot readers give an opposite meaning to an upside-down card. This practice is not followed, and you should turn all the images upwards.

If we follow these guide-lines we can then try combining cards together. When two cards are put together, your mind is forced to make a connection between them. The spark, maybe, ignites the gases from the subconscious. At a later stage we will be creating spreads and introducing the element of chance by shuffling, but at Exercise 2 it is suggested that you combine cards face *upwards* in sequences that reflect your own needs and impulses and feelings.

Two analogies are presented. Think of them as combining colours. Blue and yellow makes green. Mixing in the whole palette will produce a brown sludge. Thus, initially anyway, find meaning in only two or three cards together. Or in cooking, if you pour in the whole kitchen cabinet, you won't get the sharp flavours you'd get by combining two or them. So it is suggested you select those cards you find meaningful and start pairing them or tripling them in left/right or above/below patterns.

Perhaps A had a constricted childhood. A might select Home and Prison alongside. B has fears about health and might put the Beast alongside the Body. C hopes for a wedding and might put the Union Card above the Libido Card. D is worried about work, associating his boss with the Liar and hopes for another job. The Work Card goes on the left, the Liar underneath, Liberation goes on top ... or maybe if it's more in the future, to the right.

And so on. You play with the cards and make patterns that reflect your current situation and your hopes and fears and desires. Make a pattern of the characters and forces governing those people who matter to you.

The 'Decision' Cards, Yes, No, Now, Never and the Puzzle Card can be used as punctuation in a sequence of cards. 'Yes' encourages you to go along the train of thought. 'No' and 'Never' stops that route. 'Now' asks you to focus on the immediate and the 'Puzzle' can be treated like a question mark that asks you to stop and think.

In this second exercise you have made links between cards, creating little chains of meaning that relate to various aspects of your life.

Exercise 3: Visualising

The mysterious and beautiful wall paintings of animals in the inner darkness of caves of our hunting ancestors some 30,000 years ago can perhaps be seen as a form of visualisation.

Visualisation too has been used when the visions of heaven and hell were painted or etched in the frescos and stained glass windows of our churches to move the hearts and minds of the godly. The images in advertising make things happen in the outside world i.e. makes tills ring. Visualisation is the power of positive thinking – in image terms. There is evidence it works in practical and personal ways. By concentrating on positive forces winning over negative forces within our bodies in the shape of specific pictures we can mobilise our determination for health to overcome sickness. A graphic icon can focus the energies in our head and what happens in the head changes what happens in the outside world.

Psycards provide us the tools to steer our psychic shapes into directions we seek. The beauty and the simplicity of the cards can etch themselves in our minds and strengthen our determination to achieve our goals.

Therefore you need to create a shape with the cards that reflects your aspirations, in order to strengthen your will to make it happen.

An example. E is lonely. She had an unhappy relationship with her family who preferred her younger sister and now feels she is in a dead end job. She is however a natural linguist and decides she ought to train to get a job abroad where she might meet a new circle of friends.

After working with Psycards she selects 7 cards. She starts with the Inquirer – she herself. To the left indicating the past, she places The Father Card and the Beauty Card which she relates to her younger sister. To the right of the Inquirer Card she places the Warrior Card to strengthen her will and then the Skills to denote her language abilities. Above the skills she paces the Stars to reinforce her ambition as it were shining over the spread. Next to the Skills she places Voyage pointing her to her future.

She has crated a shape that reflects her past and her future. As yet she has introduced no element of chance. Maybe she should. But she can use the cards to fix what is in her mind and she can concentrate on them and use her will to bring them about. Because if you want something and can visualise something you can make that something happen.

Exercise 4: The Alea

Alea is the Latin word for dice, and it denotes the introduction of 'chance' in the Psycard process. 'Aleatics' is a technique that military analysts and corporate strategists apply to planning. The US Pentagon operates it on computers to work out missile programmes. Essentially it asks the question 'What If...?' 'What if... your doorbell rang and an unknown stranger said he was your long-lost brother?' 'What if.... you won the lottery tomorrow?' 'What if... you re-married and went to live in Australia?' It makes you think. It activates parts of your mind that had perhaps gone to sleep. It opens up new avenues and options.

You can call the Alea the voice of Destiny or Blind Chance. The principle of chance or randomness is built into our Universe and we should welcome it. Cosmologists tell us this is how it came into being. Biologists teach us that species evolve by exploiting random mutations. In the same way 'Aleatics' enable us to be open to the future and to expose ourselves to mental risks, to explore blind avenues and then reject them and find more rewarding routes – and in other words shape and control our futures.

So at this stage we are going to introduce the element of chance – the alea – the 'what if?' element to some of the patterns formulated in Exercise 2. We will shuffle the cards face down, though keeping some reserved.

Take A In Exercise 2. A put the Home Card next to

the Prison Card because he felt his domestic environment was constricting. A shuffles the remaining pack of Psycards and out comes the Now Card. He says to himself 'maybe I can do something about this unhappy situation. He draws another card: The Voyage. He then thinks to himself 'Maybe I really can break away from my rotten background.

Maybe A decides: 'My destiny is to follow this course of action' and this belief reinforces his feeling. But in the sequence of cards has sown a seed. It has opened a door to an alternative world and a different sort of future.

At this stage, then it is suggested you can apply some very controlled 'aleatics' to various situations, characters and possibilities in your own life to see what is sparked off. You are forced to make imaginative connections or follow hypotheses. Some you say are silly, but one or two you say 'that could make sense'. You can see something that was staring you in the face, that you half knew all the time.

The principle of the 'Alea' or randomness (which is, of course the same in Tarot and I Ching) is best, as far as Psycards are concerned, rationed. Treat the 'Alea' as a powerful drug. If you apply it too freely, it is not helpful. A in our model might unwisely draw another card: The Beast. He may surmise about the terrors of the Voyage and end up doing nothing.

Psycards also suggests that with the 'Alea' you should also be free to reject the implication of the cards as not relevant or helpful to your own situation. If it does not ring bells with you, pick another card.

Exercise 5: The Questioning
Part I

This is a technique that seeks to bring clarity to making decisions when a lot of complex emotional issues are involved. It asks you to pose some questions to the cards.

Emotional distress and uncertainty is all too similar to physical distress. When we have flu we ache all over and cannot isolate where the pain is coming from. Stress and anxiety spreads too to all departments of our lives. Then specific anxiety triggers off minor worries and reignites past doubts and the infection spreads into a miserable gloom.

Maybe in these situations you can use Psycards to see an overall shape to your life and you can see a pattern and a logic to your problems. Below are some spreads to help you do this. But in this section Psycards suggests you also apply a questioning technique. You analyse or break down your feelings into separate compartments.

It asks you to apply some analytical thinking, and it is based on the principle that you can only get good answers to problems if you ask good questions.

An example. John is going to the pub. Jane is worried. She asks herself a whole lot of different questions.

Will John be back soon?

Why is John going now when she'd like to have a talk?

Whom is he meeting? Ought John to go to the Pub? Isn't it time John broke the pub habit? What causes John to go to the Pub? Why is she so worried?

No. 1 is a factual question and time will tell. No 2 is a question about his sensitivity to her feelings. No 3 is a factual question but it prompts the additional question: is Jane jealous? No 4 is a question about morality – and prompts questions about their relationship. Nos 5 and 6 are questions about John's underlying character and past.

And No 7 is about Jane. In most complex situations there are a number of questions and issues bundled up together. Psycards suggests you break them down with three or four cards relevant to each question and leave them as questions, using the Puzzle Card as if it were a question mark. In No 1 Jane might select the Warrior Card (for John) and the Friends (for the pub) with the Puzzle Card as the question mark. In No 2 she might add the Home (she wanted him perhaps to do some DIY). In No3 she might substitute that with the Beauty (the girl behind the bar).In No 4 maybe she puts in the Scales to denote the moral question.. In No 6 she thinks John was badly brought up by his mother so she introduces the Mother Card. And for No 7 she needs some other cards that reflect her own situation.

Now Jane may not have any answers but she is perhaps clearer in her own mind about why exactly she is worried, and if you can pin down a worry you can very often do something about it. In this example Jane is questioning the cards with specific sorts of questions. Next we see the Cards questioning Jane.

Exercise 6: The Questioning
Part II

Up to now the principle of Chance or 'Aleatics' has not occurred. The cards have been specially selected by Jane in the format of three or four cards each ending up with the Puzzle Card. Now it is time to introduce the remaining cards and shuffle the pack with the cards dark or face down. One by one and separately the remaining cards are placed to the right of the Puzzle Card. That card is not giving you an answer to the question. It is asking you a question. Is this card relevant to your situation ? You can deny it. But while you are doing it you are racking your brains as to how it might fit. In the process you stretch your mindset. You introduce new thoughts. You open doors. You introduce the unconscious into the equation. It is like doing a crossword and you have the letters B A S – and you go through the alphabet to see if E or H or K fits the clue better.

In the example with Jane on No 1 she is fairly sure that John will come back – drunk. She might pre-select the Now, Never, Yes (for within an hour) No (not for within an hour) on the basis that they are the only ones relevant. She shuffles them. If Never comes up it makes Jane think how much or little she would care. That is helpful to her.

When she gets down to Question 5,which centres

on their relationship, she turns up all the cards one by one. In most cases she denies there is any relevance. But when the Union Card comes up she says to herself, ' Yes, however imperfect he is, I would like to marry him'. Or maybe, when the Destruction Card comes up, she realises there is not much hope for them together.

The Questioning process can be applied to many of the problems you face. First you ask questions for the cards. Then the cards ask questions to you .It is out of the dialogue that some answers firm up in your mind.

Exercise 7: The Spreading

Psycards encourages you to use the cards in smaller spreads rather than larger ones on the principle that you will find clearer messages with fewer cards – until you have acquired a fluency in the language of Psycards and to see a logic and a pattern in wide embracing and complex spreads. Remember too that one or two cards have an undiluted power on the Inquirer whereas six or seven cards can muddy the message.

In many cases it is suggested you treat the Inquirer as You, the person seeking the answers, and you place it face up in the centre of your spread and that the nearest influences to it will be the strongest.

As a rule on a grid system or rectilinear spreads you follow the patters of reading from left to right as past present and future with underlying and unconscious influences beneath the Inquirer. That to which the Inquirer aspires goes above. On circular spreads the Inquirer is in the centre and the cards placed around it like the planets.

Psycards suggest you use the 'aleatic' or random principle in a controlled way mixing them with cards you place in advance face upwards.

1. The Vital Seven

Place the Inquirer upright in the centre. Shuffle the pack. Lay two cards dark (i.e. face down) above, one to the left, one to the right and two below. Turn them over.

Card 2 and 3 will be goals and aspirations. Card 4 influence from the past. Card 5 the outcome in the future. Card 6 and 7 underlying and unconscious forces.

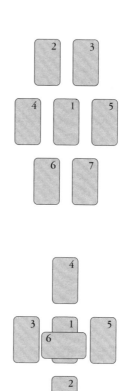

2. The Cross

Place the Inquirer (Card 1) upright in the centre. Place dark Cards 2,3,4,5, from the six o'clock position clockwise. Place Card 6 dark on top horizontal on the Inquirer.

Turn them over and read them as 2 as the underlying/unconscious, 3 as the past, 4 as your aspiration, 5 as the future and 6 as the key to the problem.

3. The See Saw

This is a spread for making Yes/No decisions or tipping the balance in

different situations where you are in two minds. You treat the Inquirer (Card 1) as the base or the fulcrum of the See Saw. On top of it you place face upward the Puzzle Card (Card 2) and on either side of it two cards (3 and 4) face upward that you select as relevant to the decision you are making. (On the example of John and Jane maybe Jane could say to John 'Let the cards decide whether you go to the pub or do the d.i.y.' She would then put the Friends Card as 3 and the Home as 4) Then shuffle the remaining cards and one by one turn them on the left and the right in Card position 5 and 6. Go on turning them over till on one side or the other a Yes or No Card appears to tilt the balance.

4. The Signpost

You are at a cross-roads and looking for where to go next. Place the Inquirer as the post of the Signpost. Shuffle the cards and place five cards face down in a North East Direction, five in a North West Direction, and five in a South Direction. The three signs will give you three alternative directions to choose from with some of the cards denoting some of the eventualities you might meet on that route. Your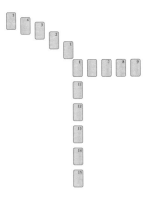

choose from with some of the cards denoting some of the eventualities you might meet on that route. Your intuition will tell you which is the most interesting and rewarding for you.

5. The Noughts and Crosses Grid

This pattern enables you to find connections with different elements of your life. (You may wish to select those cards which are most meaningful to you) You shuffle the cards and place them in three rows in a square of 9 cards. Your aim is to see a clear sequence of three cards

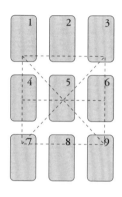

horizontally, vertically or diagonally, that make a meaningful progression of past present or future in your life.

6. Week Ahead or Year Ahead

This is a spread to prepare you for the week or year. You place the Inquirer in the centre. Starting from the Twelve O'clock position place the seven cards for the week (or 12 for the year) face down. Turn them up one by one. The Card in the Two O'clock position will alert you to what is liable to happen on, for instance, Tuesday.

7. Heart-Chart

In this spread (as on the previous one) you give a fixed position for certain 'houses' or aspects which the cards or influences, working in a clock face format. The Inquirer lies in the centre and the 7 cards on the circumference. On each of the 7 cards you place then a further card horizontally on top of it to indicate either further influence or a barrier or obstacle.

Card Position

1	Past/ Background	Hoping
2	Home	Seeking
3	Family	Fearing
4	Work	Working
5	Health	Hiding
6	Heart	Losing
7	Future	Winning

You can do the same using the seven houses as indications of movement and directions as indicated in the second column. For instance the Card in Position 1 is what the Inquirer is hoping for.

8. Who's there?

This spread is one where you can use Psycards with someone else. It enables you to understand something of what makes

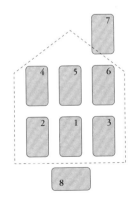

someone tick. Here you play, as it were a little 'Knock Knock' game to see who is inside the little House of the Personality and discover what their inner character is and what motivates them.

It is suggested that first you ask the person to select eight cards which they think are the most relevant to them to fill the House Shape. They place at the door: 1 the card that most represents them. At 2 what they hope for their home. At 3 their hopes for their work. At 4 their hopes for their friends, at 5 their love life, at 6 their family. At 7 how they see their future. And at 8 their fears.

All this is done with cards face upwards. The person has positioned the cards as wished. Finally you do it with all the cards dark and shuffled.

The revealing game can indicate the contrast between the perception of him/herself thrown up by the reader and by the random cards.

9. The Onion

This is a spread where an experienced psychic can see an overall pattern. It demands high levels of intuition to embrace a wide range of cards and extract from it in meaningful patterns. Think of it as an onion with different layers to reveal an inner core.

Place the Inquirer face up in the centre.(1) Shuffle and place dark nine cards as the inner ring starting in Position 2 at 12 o'clock, denoting in 2 Inward Character, Position 3 Past Success, Position 4 Past relationship, Position 5 Family Background. Position 6 Education, Position 7 Spiritual Roots, Position 8 Secret Dreams, Position 9 Inner Weakness, Position 10 Inner Strengths.

As the outer layer place downwards in Position 11 Your current driving force, Position12 Your emotional side, Position 13 Spiritual Aspirations, Position 14 Obstacles to your path, Position 15 Your work and finances, Position 16 How the world sees you, Position 17 Your Connections, Position 18 Your forgotten abilities, Position 19 Your next challenge. Position 20 Your neglected side.

In Position 21 place the final card horizontally on the No 1 and this denotes Your Future.

10. The Tapestry

This final spread uses all the cards in the Psycard pack. Shuffle the pack. Deal them in eight vertical rows of five. The reader sees a complete array of cards spread and reads them in lines going down and diagonally. Note where the Inquirer is placed and start reading from there. Look for sequences and connections. This pattern is used by Malcolm Wright of Somerset in his readings.

Exercise 8: Keep Fit for the Psyche

At a keep-fit class we will work through a disciplined routine to stretch lazy muscles and blow away our body's cobwebs. Our whole system is tuned up and we enjoy a new balance and harmony. We come out glowing and at peace.

Our hearts and minds need disciplines too. Psycards can do this because they mirror all aspects of the psyche and are a sensitive tool to help us diagnose one of the main causes of psychic aches and pains: guilt.

Our grandparents might have called it sin. If they were religious they might have 'examined their consciences'. If they were Roman Catholics they might have confessed to the priest. 'We have done those things we ought not to have done and left undone those things we ought to have done.' Few of us have corpses buried in our gardens, but pervasive guilt can nag us – about not going back to parents and friends, about bad temper and cream cakes and the mess in the hall cupboard. The worst inner voices are those that whine to us that we have failed ourselves: that our talents are rotting away or our inner growth is stunted. The most dangerous sort of guilt is when it is not overtly recognised, when it glides under the surface like a shark to savage other aspects of our life.

Psycards can help us nail the cancer of guilt by a catechism – a question & answer checklist to your personal life. In the Informing Exercise you will have put a personal value on certain cards (maybe The Warrior is your partner). In this way it is suggested you go through each relevant card and ask questions of it.

Have I done my duty to my talents?
(The Skill Card)
Have I done my duty to my body?
(The Body Card)
Have I done my duty to my intuitive skills?
(The Moon Card)
Have I done my duty to my marriage?
(The Union Card)

And so on. In some cases we can say Not Guilty. In others we admit failure. Psycards can provide no absolution, but putting the card in question next to the Peace Card can be an outward and visible sign that your failure is admitted and accepted and dissolved into the spiritual.

Excercise 9: Meditating with Psycards

Meditation is a term for the altered states of consciousness which are produced by exercises, the spoken word, or picture patterns such as Manadalas. Meditation demands discipline and it needs to be practised regularly and persistently if the subject is to achieve higher states. It has no religious connotations, no age barriers or intelligence requirements. It is performed world-wide and offers many advantages: inner peace, mental control, emotional stability, spiritual awareness, psychic awareness and a regression to suppressed or submerged memories.

Psycards are one excellent tool to use in meditation which essentially means focusing and concentrating on a specific function like breathing or a phrase, or chant or a picture. The Psycard images are an excellent focus point for your meditation programme. The colour patterns are designed to evoke moods and feelings.The images are timeless. In order to use Psycards as a meditation, time and freedom from interruptions like telephones and visitors are essential.

It is suggested you pick a selection of cards for five minutes each and feel yourself inside the picture. You are asked to bathe yourself in the colours. Here are some of the cards that may be helpful.

The Inquirer Card

Allow your eyes to drop into the pattern, focus on yourself; let your questioning dissolve away minute by minute onto the colours and shapes.

The Body Card

Use the Body Card to go within yourself. Look closely at the design and work from the toes upwards moving from the card to your own toes. Move slowly up the flanks of the body, looking for dis-ease, and tension. Move through the card and through your own body so that peace and energy radiates through all your channels.

The Money Card

Go for a walk with the Money Card. Imagine you are the farmer ploughing his field hour by hour furrow by furrow. Look around at the bare trees and the sky and feel the texture of the earth.

Friendship Card

Imagine you are in the tavern with the friends. think of what the characters are talking about. Surmise what is their relationship. Is there a hint of jealousy between them? Who is the next person to walk in?

What is the parrot saying? Lose yourself inside that tavern for five minutes and you will come out refreshed.

Birth Card

With this card allow yourself to become the earth and feel the energy flowing from below from above from the dew. Sense the sunlight and the new life seeping into the cells.

The Peace Card

At times there is a need to go within yourself and find God. So gaze at this card a while before you close your eyes. Think of yourself in the vaulted central space of a cathedral and see the sunlight shafting into the stone. As you do it you hear a distant choir singing and that you are filled sometimes with inner peace and tranquillity.

Exercise 10: Soul matching

People are lonely. As the bonds of traditional families, mainline religions and secure jobs loosen we become atomised. We want to know who we are and we look to the loadstone of a meaningful personal relationship to shape our lives. How can we find soul mates, people with whom we have affinities, with whom we can really talk? (because we know between people what is in the head is as important and closely linked to what is in the bed)

The trouble is that people don't come with attractive transparent supermarket wrapping. WYSIWYG (What you see is what you get) isn't true in personal relationships. Many of us find it hard to talk about ourselves or drop psychical defences .

Psycards can help us select compatible partners, indeed soul mates. They have been used more and more with people who have met through dating and intro-ductory agencies, but they can also be helpful to any couple who seek to explore deeper into each others' feelings .

The exercise is simple. You go through the 40 cards with your partner and vice versa. You ask in particular

What associations/feelings does this card have for you?

What hopes does it offer you?

What fears does it present to you?

It should be done fast, passing over blockages, but it allows you to touch on deeply based personal feelings.

Pictures can act as prompt cards for talking about taboo areas that words cannot. We often have little time to find out whether a stranger is compatible and the 40 cards are a better guide to discover more about another person than their reactions to yesterday's TV.

Psycards and Counselling

Therapists and Counsellors have multiplied in the last decade. The number of them , whatever discipline or training they may have, must indicate they are responding to the needs and demands of their clients. This is understandable. People feel they have a right to be happy, yet life is difficult. Recession, divorce, unemployment, stress deprives them of their right. There are fewer role models. Vicars and wise aunties are hard to find. People want other people to talk to in an atomised society. As problems mount so there are sensitive and sensible people who want to help. Some of them may not have a proper training but they have a fund of wisdom and experience as well as 'people skills'. Both to those people and a very wide range of trained qualified practising therapists the Psycards system is highly relevant.

Psycards enable an individual to find a shape (or configuration or gestalt) out of the disparate elements of his/her life and make sense of them and the counsellor's role is to facilitate the process. In any humanistic model a change of behaviour can only come from a change in the client's perception and understanding through the willing realignment of the self, the I, the Inquirer.

Counselling is 99% talking and many people lack the vocabulary to talk about their inner landscape. In a world which is getting more and more visual and less discursive, a language of open-ended symbols can support and lubricate the process. The cards can act as pegs and prompts and highlight areas that the client is unwilling to broach. They can speed up the therapy process - no small achievement in what is a labour intensive industry.

Counselling with Psycards has to be client-centred and non-directional - diametrically different from the 'reader' who 'predicts' a client's future. The cards allow the client to talk through his/her problems in protected space where the self is not threatened. The counsellor is not suggesting or prompting outside values and not criticising or moralising.

He/she encourages the client to play with the cards and build connections and shapes and find their own directions and explore their inner world. In any session the client is 're-organising' the self, shaping it in a way that is more coherent and congruent to reality. He/she can relax and explore new self-models creating 'what if' scenarios with the alea. New threatening material is explored tentatively. The client can reject unwelcome patterns and the goal throughout is to allow the client control and to find a safe space for the self to grow in confidence. In this process the counsellor is a co-worker.

This of course reflects Carl Rogers client-centred counselling theory. But it is compatible with many psychotherapeutic schools and thinking. In the Gestalt school the primary therapeutic tool is the development of awareness within the self thereby helping the client to get in touch with him/herself. Shorr in1972 developed a technique of Psycho Imagination using the client's conscious imagery as a systematic tool (indeed he outlines the technique of 'questioning')

Agassio highlights the importance of symbol utilisation in the dynamics of the psyche and the Psycard system with its Jungian bias reflects the whole direction of Psychosynthesis with the self reaching up to a higher self. Psycards are therefore useful versatile tools for therapists and analysts in a wide spectrum of humanistic and psychodynamic disciplines.

For the layman counselling with Psycards too has a role as long as a clear distinction can be made.It has been accepted from time immemorial that some people have psychic gifts, an 'uncanny' insight into other people's lives. For these ' seers' Psycards are a useful medium. But counselling demands another gift from the psyche: empathy and sensitivity. It is to enable the client to 'see' his/her own future, not tell it for him/her. It means letting the client find his/her own meaning in the cards and make shapes and directions. The client is on a journey and the counsellor is a guide and companion - as Virgil was to Dante as he entered the underworld.

A Psycards Case History

Jean is 39. She is an art-director in a publisher's studio. She has a daughter of six, is separated from her husband. She now lives with a man friend from work. She's restless and unsatisfied with her work and her domestic situation. A friend worked with Psycards with her.

In the Informing Stage Jean related specific cards to her situation.

The Stars for her daughter (who was named Estelle)

The Beauty Card for her artistic talent and her self.

The Tower for her lover – largely for the reason he was tall.

The Home for her whole domestic situation.

The Work Card for her job.

She did a Questioning Exercise and random spreads centred on those specific cards.

As to the Work Card she was puzzled why the Liar Card fell to the left of the Beauty Card, and the Destruction Card the other side. On consideration she found it significant and reminded her that how much she basically disliked the trashy work she was doing and that she was wasting her talent.

As to the Stars Card when The Father came up, it brought to mind how much her daughter needed a satisfactory father relationship.

In the Tower Card, when the Mother Card was recurring it alerted her to the possibility that her lover was treating her as a mother figure which she did not want to fulfil.

As to the Home Card she wondered what the significance of The Stranger which appeared prominently in three spreads. She interpreted it as her estranged ex-husband.

Working with the Cards Jean became clearer in her mind that she was missing her ex-husband with whom she had decided to break originally. She now felt she should leave her job and her lover. She found strength in visualising a sequence of cards: Beauty, Stars, Stranger, Home, Union.

The Cards had helped her find peace and clarity of mind and achieve the purpose energy and confidence to seek a closer relationship with her ex-husband.

To the Reader

Probably round the world some 20,000 people use Psycards. They do so in a wide variety of ways: as a more user-friendly less spooky sort of Tarot, as prompts to creativity and story-telling, as tools for personal development and as patient aids in clinical psychotherapy.

The author of this book would like to know about your ideas comments and criticisms, including the meanings you give to the cards, how you use them and any interesting case histories.

Psycards is very much a developing and open-ended system and you input would be helpful for other users.

PSYCARDS